WHAT THE THREE AS ONE REVEALED TO ME

WHAT THE THREE AS ONE REVEALED TO ME

(A SPIRITUAL JOURNEY)

PHYLLIS AMES-BEY

Published in the United States of America

ISBN 978-1-962730-08-2 (SC)

Library of Congress Control number 2022901001

Phyllis Ames-Bey Publishing
222 West 6th Street
Suite 400, San Pedro, CA, 90731
www.stellarliterary.com

Order Information and Rights Permission:

Quantity sales. Special discounts might be available on quantity purchases by corporations, associations, and others. For details, contact the publisher at the address above.

For Book Rights Adaptation and other Rights Permission.
Call us at toll-free 1-888-945-8513 or send us an email at
admin@stellarliterary.com.

Contents

Dedication

Giving Honor to ABBA FATHER, I truly thank Him for the partial completion of this book. It was His dedicating Spirit within me which enabled me to complete putting it together within 24 hours with the help of a social media I am a member of.

I wish to dedicate this book to my son, Saleem E. Ali-Bey for his love, support and understanding. I also wish to dedicate it to my mentor and very close friend Bishop B. B. Brown; my prayer warriors Wanda Cauley, Joan Hamilton-Ginns, Gisel Barksdale, Karen and Phoebe and our other prayer intercessors on our Webbex prayer line.

Last but not least, I dedicate the book to my sisters Estella Hickmond and Belinda Hoffman-bey, my Spiritual daughter and son Yolanda & Joseph Young-bey and my grands and great grands, and my friend of 23 years-Darryl Butcher.

Acknowledgements

Again, I thank my friend and Spiritual Mentor Bishop B. B. Brown and my son Saleem for helping me gather additional knowledge, understanding and wisdom.

I thank the Young-Beys for elevating my son to Divine Minister and State Grand Sheik of Pennsylvania. I also wish to thank Supreme Grand Governor Robert Stone-El, Divine Minister and the Grand Body for the appointment of my son Sheik Saleem Ali-Bey as the Grand Governor of Pennsylvania and Joseph and Yolanda Young-Bey as Regional Grand Governor and Assistant Regional Grand Governor of the State of New York.

My Next book will be Grace, Goodness and Mercy of Abba Father. This book will contain Phyllis Personal Prayers.

Introduction

I GATHERED THE WRITINGS OF OVER A 7 YEAR PERIOD ON 11/21/21 AND COMPLETED THE PROCESS ON 11/22/21 WITH THE HELP OF MY SOCIAL MEDIA.

THIS BOOK CONSIST OF ARTICLES OF MY RELATIONSHIP WITH ABBA FATHER, JESUS AND THE HOLY GHOST SPIRIT AS ONE ENTITY. IT GIVES INFORMATION ON HOW THE SCRIPTURES AFFECTED ME AND CAUSED ME TO WANT TO SHARE THOSE EXPERIENCES.

Song To Abba
Father Jehovah

Father, thank you for Your breath we breathe, We thank You for everything while on our knees.
Thank you for the blood which was shed, Thank You for allowing us to be led
By Your son Jesus Christ our savior Thank You for all of the favor
You've given to us by Your grace, Thank You for allowing us to see your face.
Abba Father, continue holding our hands as we faithfully walk throughout this land
Keep a hedge of protection around us all, continue holding us so that we won't fall
This I ask in Jesus name Yes I am without feeling shame
Thank you Father, for Your love. Thank you for blessings from above.

by phyllis ames-bey

My All Is On The Altar

You know, no matter who or what I am I belong to my Lord God Jesus
Christ
For He is the one who choose me I am His-the rest of my life.
Lord Jesus hear the words in my heart while in this seat I pray
know the truth of my new start know with you I will stay and obey.
I will praise and worship you my GOD, all night and all the day long
You are the Most High Holy King I will write about you in song.
Jesus you are the bread of my life I am yours with no stress or strife
I magnify your Holy name for you always remain the same.

I yield my body and my soul and leave a lot of words untold
You know all about me when I am hot, lukewarm or cold.
Lord Jesus You are my all in all Yours is the love I claim
Thanks for allowing me to answer the call, for You were always my aim.
I thank Joan and Bishop B B Brown for guiding me back home to You
Continue guiding my footstep and letting me see I must include You in all I
do.
Lord Jesus I belong to You, I give you my all and all
Let your Spirit dwell within me hold me up so I don't fall

Remove all fear, fill me with faith and anointing power too
Help me to minister Your good word in all I say and do
bless and fill me with Your love as You reach down from above
Lift me up my Lord and let me stay in Your arms all the time with LOVE.

by phyllis ames-bey

1 Reason Why Your Life Is As It Is

Created on 2016-12-08 07:28

It is written in James 4:2 **Ye have not because ye ask not. Jesus said in Luke 11:9 I say unto you ask and it shall be given, seek and ye shall find, knock and it shall be opened unto you. Ask for what you want in the name of JESUS. Remember Matthew 18:19-20 Again I say unto you, that if two of you shall agree on earth as touching anything that they shall ask, it shall be done for them of my Father which is in heaven. For where two or three are gathered together in my name, there am I in the midst of them. Have faith with works. Believe. Faith without works is dead. In Hebrews 11:6 without faith it is impossible to please HIM, for he that cometh to GOD MUST BELIEVE THAT HE IS, and THAT HE is a rewarder of them that diligently SEEK HIM.**

Understand, **Jesus went back to the Father so** the **Comforter** could come to us. **John 16:6-16 Jesus said-I tell you the truth- it is expedient for you that I go away; for if I go NOT away the Comforter will not come unto you; but if I depart, I will send Him unto you. I have many things to say unto you but you can not bear them now. When He, the Spirit of Truth is come, he will guide you unto all truth for he will speak NOT of himself; but whatsoever he shall hear, that shall he speak and he will show you things to come.**

He **shall glorify me; for he shall receive of mine, and show it unto you. All things that the Father have are MINE, therefore said I, that he shall take of mine and show it unto you. I go to the Father.**

The Lord is merciful and gracious, slow to anger and plenteous in mercy. He will not always chide, neither will He keep His anger for ever. He hath not dealt with us after our sins, nor rewarded us according to our iniquities. **For as the heaven is high above the earth, so Great is His mercy toward them that fear Him. As far as the east is from the west, so far hath He removed our transgressions from us. Like as a father pitieth his children so the Lord pitieth them that fear Him, for He knoweth our frame, He remember that we are dust. The mercy of God is from everlasting to everlasting upon them that fear Him and His righteousness unto children's children; to such as keep His covenant and to those that remember His commandments and to do them. One of those commandments is to LOVE ONE ANOTHER AS I HAVE LOVED YOU.**

Bless the Lord, all his works in all places of His dominion, Bless the Lord O my soul. Psalm 103. Lets finish this by praying THE LORD'S PRAYER-the perfect prayer that JESUS taught us to pray to Our Father.

A Little Metaphysical Spirituality

Created on 2016-11-28 09:43

Because religions accept various beliefs on faith, they are metaphysical. Truth is truth no matter what or who you follow. Jesus followed and taught the teachings of Essenes. It included the practice of discipline of meditation, healing and communication with God, who is The Father, the divine source of all power. Jesus taught a very pure religion. I have to ask you not to mix religion up with a belief system. Jesus is a Spiritual Being. And we are the body of Christ, made up of many members, going through human experiences to learn from those experiences so that we can grow spiritually. We are co-creators with the Divine, Supreme Being, who is God, our father. We also learn and love.

But **know this, God is love and love is GOD IN MANIFESTATION.** Love is the creative source **spiritually of all creation. We must always be conscious of our thoughts, words and actions for we are directing energy to manifest in the ether, our thoughts into reality. In doing so, we are creating conditions and situations in which we have to make decisions on. Then you have to use free will power and hope you made the right choice in the situation or condition you created because you reap what you sow.**

Metaphysics is the nature of reality. **Jesus, who is a reality (to me spiritually anyway) said greater things than He, we shall be able to do. I am going to ask a question-are ye gods? Is it a sin to say you are? Do you know what sin is? I read it was actions and thoughts in violation with Spiritual**

Law. God dwell in me and me in Jesus and Jesus in The Father. I am god-like for he told us to be fruitful and multiply. He gave us the ability to create. Out of love, my son was manifested. And the fruits from my tree are many, beautiful, wonderful blessings of grands because of him. Again I ask, does that make us a god, because we are co-creators of this world with God, Our Father. We should be praising, thanking worshiping Him and giving God glory for making us who we are. Man should not glory in man, for as per 1 Corinthians 3:21-22, all things are ours, the world, life, death, things present or things to come all are ours and we are Christ's and Christ is God's.

We are the temple of God. Every man shall receive his own reward according to his own labor, for we are laborers together with God and we are God's building. The Foundation is Jesus Christ. Read 1 Corinthians 3:1-23 Also read the Spiritual Laws of Metaphysical Spirituality, and what it says about each law. Read about: The Law of Life, The Law of Truth, The Law of Compensation, The Law of Attraction, The Law of Abundance, The Law of Freedom, The Law of Love and the Law of Perfection. Now I know some of you are saying we don't live under the law anymore because Jesus died for us. These are not the same laws. There is a difference between the laws of Caesar or man or the old testaments and these laws which Jesus taught about. Especially the law of love. We are here to love, create, learn from experiences to enable us to grow Spiritually. Read all the books you can read, The Bible, the Koran, the Circle 7, Metaphysics, etc. etc. Pray the Lord's Prayer today and every day. Jesus taught us that prayer and told us to pray it when we pray. God bless each and every one of you.

Are You Renouncing
The Will Of God

Created on 2016-09-11 11:49

Romans 1:17 The just shall live by faith. Galatians 3:26 Ye are all children of God by faith in Christ Jesus. God has shown man the truth. Just what did He say about those renouncing His will and turning to idolatry? What did He say about heterosexuality verses homosexuality? I am not being judgemental or trying to tell you how to live. But know there are consequences for every decision you make be it positive or negative. Here is some knowledgeable reading for you to try to understand and gain wisdom from.

Galatians 5:16-25 Walk in the spirit and ye shall not fulfill the lust of the flesh. The works of the flesh are manifested. SEE Galatians 5:19-21 which explains what the works are. They which do such things will not inherit the kingdom of God. But the fruit of the Spirit is love, joy, peace, longsuffering, gentleness, goodness, faith, meekness, temperance against such there is no law. And they that are Christ's have crucified the flesh with the affections and love. If we live in the Spirit, let us also walk in the Spirit.

Romans 1:18-32 The wrath of God is revealed from heaven against all ungodliness and unrighteousness of men who hold the truth in unrighteousness: because that which may be known of God is manifest in them for God has shown it unto them. For the invisible things of Him are clearly seen, being understood by the things that are made, even His external power and Godhead: so that they are without excuse: because when they knew God, they glorified Him not as God, neither were thankful, but became vain in their imaginations, and their foolish heart was darkened. Professing themselves to be wise they became fools and changed the glory of an uncorruptible God into an image made like to corruptible man, and to birds, and fourfooted beasts and creeping things, wherefore God also gave them up to uncleanness through the lusts of their own hearts, to dishonor their own bodies between themselves: Who changed the truth of God into a lie and worshipped and served the creature more than the Creator, who is blessed forever. AMEN. For this cause (they were idol worshipers) God gave them up unto vile affections; for even their women change the natural use into that which is against nature and likewise also the men leaving the natural use of the woman, burned in their lust one towards another: men with men working that which is unseemly, and receiving in themselves that recompense of their ERROR which was meet. (Is this homosexuality?) And even as they did not like to retain God in THEIR knowledge. God gave them over to a reprobate mind, to do those things which are not convenient, being filled with all unrighteousness. Please see what they were in vs 29-32.

But we who walk in the Spirit have peace with God. We have hope in God. And hope maketh not ashame because the love of God is spread abroad in our hearts by the Holy Ghost which is given unto us. (Romans 5:5) Romans 5:19 For as one man's disobedience many were made sinners, so by the obedience of ONE shall many be made righteous. Romans 6:12-13 Let not sin therefore reign in your mortal body, that ye shall obey it in the lusts thereof. Neither yield ye your members as instruments of unrighteousness unto sin but yield yourselves unto God, and those that are alive from the dead and your members as instruments of righteousness unto God.

I will close by asking you to pray the Lord's Prayer today. For thine is the Kingdom, and the power and the glory, forever and ever and ever and ever. Amen and thank God.

Being A Soldier
In God's Army

Created on 2017-12-28 11:38

While being in God's army, put on the whole armor of God. Eph 6:12 For we wrestle not against flesh and blood, but against principalities, against powers, against the rulers of the darkness of this world, against spiritual wickedness in high places. But remember, greater is He that is within you so put on the whole armor of God. Eph 6:13-18 Stand therefore, having your loins girt about with truth, and having on the breastplate of righteousness, and your feet shod with the preparation of the gospel of peace, above all taking the shield of faith, wherewith ye shall be able to quench all the fiery darts of the wicked: and take the helmet of salvation and the sword of the Spirit, which is the Word of God. Praying always with all prayer and supplication in the Spirit, for you have the victory. Zech 4:6 not by might, not by power but by my Spirit saith the Lord of Hosts. Ps 31:24 Be of good courage and He shall strengthen your heart, all ye that hope in the Lord. For the Lord is our hope, He is our trust from our youth. (Ps 71:5) 2 Cor 2:14 Thanks be unto God, which always causeth us to triumph in Christ.

Ps 25:10, 9 All the paths of the Lord are mercy and truth unto such as keep His covenant and His testimonies. The meek will He guide in judgment; and the meek will He teach His way. Ps 32:8 God said He will instruct you and teach you in the way which thou shall go. He will guide you with His eye. Ps 54:4 In God-praise His Word. In God-put your trust. Do not fear what flesh can do unto you. Prov 18:10 The name of the Lord is a strong tower, The righteous runneth into it and is safe. Is 41:13 The Lord God is holding your right hand. He is saying unto you, fear not, I will help thee. Is 41:10-11 Fear not, for I am with thee, be not dismayed, for I am thy God, I will strengthen thee: yea, I will help thee; yea, I will uphold thee with the right hand of my righteousness, all those that were against thee shall be ashamed and confounded. They shall be as nothing and they that strive with thee shall perish.

Ps 91:9-12 Because thou hast made the Lord which is my refuge, even the Most High thy habitation, there shall no evil befall thee neither shall any plague come nigh thy dwelling, for He shall give His angels charge over thee, to keep thee in all thy ways. They shall bear thee up in their hands lest thou dash thy foot against a stone. Gen 14:20 Blessed be the Most High God which hath delivered thine enemies into thine hand. Read all of the 91st Psalm from 1-16 for protection. Also pray the Lord's Prayer today. May all the readers be blessed and have a safe, healthy, prosperous New Year while allowing the Spirit of Jesus dwell within them. Abba Father know no limits and does not have limits on Him. He will bless us abundantly. Amen and Amen.

Being Healed Spiritually As Well As Physically And Mentally

Created on 2016-07-18 08:30

Romans 5:3-5 We glory in tribulations also knowing with tribulations, we have patience and patience, experiences, and experiences, hope, and hope maketh not ashamed because the love of God is shed abroad in our hearts by the Holy Ghost which is given unto us. 1 Corinthians 12:8-10 For to us is given by the Spirit the word of wisdom, and to another the word of knowledge by the same Spirit, to another faith by the same Spirit, to another the working of miracles, to another prophecy, to another discerning spirits, to another, divers kind of tongue, to another the interpretation of tongues. But all that worketh, that one and the selfsame Spirit, dividing to every man severally as He may.

1 Peter 4:12, 13, 15, 16, 19 Beloved, think it not strange the fiery trial which is to try you as though some strange thing happened with you. But rejoice, in as much as ye are partakers of Christ's sufferings: that, when His glory shall be revealed, ye may be glad also with exceeding joy. But let none of you suffer as a murderer, or as a thief, or as an evildoer or as a busybody in other men's matters. Wherefore let them that suffer according to the will of God commit the keeping of their souls to him in well doing, as unto a faithful creator.

When sick and in pain allow yourself to be healed spiritually by in knowing about the spiritual references above. You will realize where your help comes from. Psalm 38:5, 6, 8, 9, 15, 21, 22 my wounds stink and are corrupt, I am troubled, I am bow down greatly. I am feeble and sore, broken. Lord, all my desire is before thee. For thee O Lord do I hope. Thou will hear, O Lord, my God. Forsake me not O Lord, oh my God, be not far from me. Make haste to help me, O Lord my salvation. This I ask in the name of Jesus. Thank you, Jesus, Amen and Amen.

Do You Despise The Church Of God

***

Created on 2016-10-10 12:7:55

We, our temples, are the church of God in Jesus Christ. Matt 16:18-19 upon this rock I will build my church and the gates of hell shall not prevail against it; and I will give unto thee the keys of the kingdom of heaven. 1 Cor 4:20 The kingdom of God is not in words but in power. Col 3:16 Let the word of Christ dwell in you richly in all wisdom; teaching and admonishing one another in psalms and hymns and spiritual songs, singing with grace in your hearts to the Lord. Ps 33:3 Sing unto Him a new song, play skillfully with a loud noise. Col 3:17 and whatsoever ye do in word or deed, do all in the name of the Lord Jesus, giving thanks to God and the Father by Him.

Acts 20:28 Take heed therefore unto yourselves, and to all the flock, over the which the Holy Ghost hath made you overseers to feed the church of God, which He hath purchased with His own blood. 1 Cor 11:22 What? have ye not houses to eat and to drink in? or despise ye the church of God and shame them that have not? What shall I say to you? 1 Cor 12:27-28 Now ye are the body of Christ and members in particular: and God hath set some in the church, first apostles, secondarily prophets, thirdly teachers after that miracles, then gifts of healing, helps, governments, diversity of tongues. 1 Cor 14:4-5 he that spoke in an unknown tongue edifieth himself; but he that prophesieth edifieth the church - greater is he that prophesieth than he that speaketh with tongues except he interpret, that the church may receive edifying.

Eph 3:9-12 The fellowship of the mystery, which from the beginning of the world hath been hid in God, who created all things by Jesus Christ to the intent that now unto the principalities and powers in heavenly places might be known by the church the manifold wisdom Of God, according to the eternal purposed in Christ Jesus our Lord, in whom we have boldness and access with confidence by the faith of Him.

You will never see the end of God's love. Eph 3:14-21 For this cause I bow my knees unto the Father of our Lord Jesus Christ, of whom the whole family in heaven and earth is named that He grant you to be strengthened with might by His Spirit in the inner man, that Christ may dwell in your hearts by faith: that ye being rooted and grounded in love to know the love of Christ which passeth knowledge, that ye might be filled with all the fullness of God. Unto be glory in the church by Christ Jesus throughout all ages, world without end. AMEN.

So, Ep 4:23-32 Be renewed in the Spirit of your mind. Put on the new man, which after God is created in righteousness and true holiness. Put away lying, speak every man truth with his neighbor; for we are members one of another. Be ye angry and sin not; let not the sun go down upon your wrath neither give place to the devil. Steal no more, labor with your hands that thing which is good that you may give to him that needeth. Let no corrupt communication proceed out of your mouth. Say what will minister grace unto the hearers. Grieve not the Holy Spirit of God. Put away all bitterness, wrath, and evil speaking and be kind one to another, tenderhearted, forgiving one another even as God for Christ sake have forgiven you. Ep 5:1-2 Be followers of God as dear children and walk in love, as Christ also hath loved us and gave Himself for us as a sacrifice to God.

Speak to God the following: Psalm 119:10-35 With my whole heart have I sought thee. Let me not wander from thy commandments. Thy word have I hid in mine heart that I might not sin against thee. Blessed art Thou O Lord, teach me thy statues. With my lips have I declared all the judgements of my mouth. I will meditate in thy precepts and have respect unto thy ways. I will delight myself in thy statues, I will not forget thy word. Remove from me reproach and contempt. I have declared my ways. Thou hearest me, teach me thy statues, make me to understand the ways of thy precepts, so shall I talk of thy wonderous works. Remove from me the way of lying. I have chosen the way of truth. Give me understanding and I shall observe it with my whole heart. Make me to go in the path of thy commandments for therein do I delight.

Our Father, which art in heaven, hallowed be Thy name, thy kingdom come, thy will be done, on earth as it is in heaven. Give us this day our daily bread, and forgive us our debts as we forgive our debtors, and lead us not into temptation, but deliver us from evil, for Thine is the kingdom, and the power and the glory, for ever and forever and forever and forever, Amen and thank God.

Do You Have Knowledge Of God

Created on 2015-12-04 09:31

Rev 19:11-JESUS is called Faithful and True. Rev 19:13 JESUS name is called the Word of God. Rev. 19:10 Worship God-for the testimony of JESUS is the spirit of prophecy.

Hosea 4:6 My people are destroyed for lack of knowledge: because thou hast rejected knowledge, I will also reject thee. God desires love, mercy and KNOWLEDGE OF HIM more than offerings. Hosea 6:6 Hear the word of the Lord, for the Lord hath a controversy with the inhabitants of the land, because there is no truth, no mercy nor KNOWLEDGE OF GOD in the land. By swearing, and lying, and killing, and stealing and committing adultery, they breakout, and blood toucheth blood. Hosea 4:1-2 Come, let us return unto the Lord. He will heal us. To receive the blessings-read Hosea 6:1-3. Return unto the Lord-take with you words-say unto Him, "take away all iniquity and receive us graciously." Hosea 14:1-2 God promises to heal. I will heal their backsliding, I will love them freely. Hosea 4:4 For the ways of the Lord are right, and the just shall walk in them.

You may find me repeating a few scriptures I previously posted, but the words are truth and knowledgeable, which you may need to try and understand. St John 1:1-3 In the beginning was the Word, and the Word was with God and the Word was God. The same was in the beginning with God. All things were made by Him, and without Him was not anything made that was made. Genesis 1-Chapter 1 In the beginning God created the heaven and the earth.

And His Spirit moved upon the face of the waters, and God spoke Words-He said let there be-and what He spoke happened-and God saw - it was good, verse 26 and God said; "Let us make man in our image after our likeness, verse 31 and God saw every thing He had made (including man) and behold it was very good and the evening and the morning were the sixth day.

Moving ahead to more knowledge-St John 1:4-14 In Him was life and that Life was the Light of men. There was a man sent from God name John who came to bear witness of that light, that all men through Him might believe that was the true Light that lighteth every man that cometh into the world. He was in the world, the world was made by Him an the world knew Him not. Not even His own received Him. But as many as received Him, to them gave he power to become the sons of God, even to them that believed on His name: which were born not of blood, nor of the will of the flesh, nor of the will of men but of God. And the Word was made flesh and dwelt among us full of grace and truth.

John 4:22-24, 26, 32, 34 Ye worship, ye know not what: but the hour cometh, and now is, when the true worshipers shall worship the Father in Spirit and Truth: for the Father seeketh such to worship Him. God is a Spirit and they that worship Him must worship Him in Spirit and in truth. A woman said unto Jesus, when the messiah come which is called Christ, he will tell us all things. Jesus said unto her, "I that speak unto thee am He." He told his disciples "I have meat to eat that ye know not of." "My meat is to do the will of Him that sent me and to finish His work."

Have you thought about what He meant when He said to finish His work? I thought about it. Remember when He said on the cross "it is finished"-He meant He finished God's work. John 3:16-21 For God so loved the world He gave his only begotten Son that whosoever believeth in Him should not perish but have everlasting life. God sent his Son, that the world through Him might be saved. He that believeth on Him is not condemned. He that believeth not is condemned because the light is come into the world and men loved darkness rather than the light. But he that doeth TRUTH cometh to the light, that his deeds may be made manifest that they are wrought in God. Check your bible. Jesus, himself spoke the words in John 3:16-21. All of the words are in red lettering. When He said it is finished-we received redemption through his blood, the forgiveness of sins, according to the riches of his grace-God-Having made know to us the mystery of his will, according to his good pleasure which he had purposed in himself; that in the dispensation of the fullness of times he might gather together in one all things in Christ, both which are in heaven, and which are on earth, even in him: in whom also we have obtained an inheritance, being predestined according to the purpose of him who worketh all things after the counsel of his own will: that we should be to the praise of his glory who first trusted in Christ. Ephesians 1:9-12

Ephesians 1:17-18 That he God of our Lord Jesus Christ, the Father of glory, nay give unto you the spirit of wisdom and revelation in the knowledge of him: the eyes of your understanding being enlightened; that ye may know what is the hope of his calling and what the riches of the glory of his inheritance in the saints. For complete knowledge of this section -read Ephesians 1:19-23.

Let these words (meat) sink into your spirit. Isa 44:6, 8 I am the first and the last: and beside me there is no God. Fear ye not, neither be afraid, have not I told you from that time, and have declared it? There is no God beside me, I know not any. Isa 45:4-7 I have even called thee by thy name: I have surnamed thee, thou hast not known me. I am the LORD and there is none else, there is no God beside me, I girded thee, though thou hast not known me. That they may know from the rising of the sun, and from the west, there is none beside me. I am the Lord and there is none else; I form the light and create darkness, I made peace and create evil, I the Lord do all these things. Isa 46:9 I am God and there is none else; I am God and there is none like me. For those of you who read the new testaments, Jesus said the first of all commandments is "Hear, the Lord our God is one Lord," and thou should love the Lord thy God with all thy heart, soul, mind and strength; it is the first commandment and the second thou shall love thy neighbor as thyself. There is none other commandments greater than these.

John 13:3 Jesus knowing that the father had given all things into his hands and that he was coming from God, went to God. John 13:20 Jesus said 'verily, verily I say unto you, he that receiveth whomsoever I send receiveth me, and he that receiveth me receiveth him that sent me, John 14:15-21 Jesus said if you love me keep my commandments and I will pray to the Father and He shall give you another Comforter, that He may abide with you forever-even the Spirit of Truth whom the world cannot receive, because it seeth Him not-neither knoweth Him; but ye knoweth Him; for he dwell with you and shall be in you. I will not leave you comfortless. I will come to you, because I live, ye shall live also. Ye shall know that I am in my father, and ye in me, and I in you. He that loveth me shall be loved of my Father, and I will love him and will manifest myself to him. Please read John 5:19-47 for additional knowledge.

Rev 21:1, 3 And I saw a new heaven and earth, and I heard a voice out of heaven saying-Behold, the tabernacle of God is with men, and He will dwell with them and they shall be his people and God himself shall be with them and be their God. For additional knowledge read Rev 21:1-7 Rev 22:7 Behold I come quickly: blessed is he that keepeth the sayings of the prophecy of this book. Rev 1:12 my reward is with me to give every man according as his work shall be. Rev 1:13 I am Alpha and Omega, the beginning and the end, the first and the last. Rev 1:14 Blessed are they that do His commandments that hey may have the right to the tree of life and may enter in through the gates into the city. Rev 1:16 I, Jesus have sent mine angel unto you to testify unto you these things in the churches. I am the root and the offspring of David, and the bright and morning star. Rev 1:20 surely I come quickly. Rev 1:8 I am Alpha and Omega, the beginning and the ending which is and which was and which is to come. The Almighty. Rev 1:11 I am Alpha and Omega, the first and the last. Rev 1:17 Fear not, I am the first and the last. I am He that liveth and wad was dead and behold I am alive for evermore, AMEN: and have the keys of hell and death. Rev 3:20 Behold, I stand at the door and knock-if any man hear my voice and open the door, I will come in to him and sup with him and he with me. To him that overcome will I grant to sit with me in my throne even as I overcame and am sat down with my Father in His throne. For knowledge please read Rev chapter 7. Read also all of 2nd Corinthians. Let us pray in closing-Matt 6:6-13 and please pay attention to verses 14 and 15 about forgiveness.

Our Father which art in heaven, Hallowed be thy name. Thy kingdom come. Thy will be done in earth as it is in heaven. Give us this day our daily bread, and forgive us our trespasses as we forgive those who trespass against us and lead us not into temptation, but deliver us from evil: for Thine is he kingdom, and the power and the glory, forever. AMEN.

Getting To Know
The God I Serve

Created on 2017-05-29 18:51

Rev 1:18 I am He that liveth and was dead; and behold I am alive forevermore, and have the keys of hell and of death. 2 Pet 3:9 The Lord is not slack concerning His promise as some men count slackness, but is longsuffering to us-ward, not willing that any should perish, but that all should come to repentance. Col 3:12 Put on therefore as the elect of God, holy and beloved bowels mercies, kindness, humbleness of mind, meekness, longsuffering. Heb 4:-12-14 for the word of God is quick and powerful and sharper than any twoedged sword piercing even to the dividing asunder of soul and spirit, and of the joints and marrow, and is a discerner of the thoughts and intents of the heart. Neither is their any creature that is not manifested in His sight; but all things are naked and opened unto the eyes of Him with whom we have to do. Seeing then that we have a great high priest that is passed into the heavens, JESUS the son of God, let us hold fast to our profession. Prov 3:34 Surely, He scorned the scorners, but He giveth grace unto the lowly.

Ps 99:9 Exalt the Lord our God, and worship at His hold hill; for the Lord our God is Holy. 2 Sam 22:2-4 The Lord is my rock, and my fortress, and my deliverer. The God of my rock; in Him will I trust for He is my shield and the horn of my salvation, my high tower, and my refuge, my savior, that savest me from violence. I will call on the Lord who is worthy to be praised so shall I be saved from mine enemies. Ps 45:7 thou loveth righteousness and hate wickedness, therefore God, thy God, hath anointed thee with the oil of gladness above the fellows. Heb 12:1-2 let us lay aside every weight and the sin which so easily beset us, and let us run with patience the race that is set before us looking unto JESUS the author and finisher of our faith who for the joy that was set before Him endured the cross, despising the shame and is set down at the right hand of the throne of God. Rev 3:12 Him that overcometh will I make a pillar in the temple of my God.. (see Rev 3:12)

Job 5:17-18 Behold happy is the man whom God correcteth; therefore despise not the chastening of the Almighty; for He maketh sore and bindeth up; He wounded and He maketh whole. Ps 147:3, 5 He health the broken in heart and bindeth up their wounds. Great is our Lord and of great power; His understanding is infinite. Rom 5:5 and hope maketh not ashamed because the love of God is shed abroad in our hearts by the Holy Ghost which is given to us. Gal 5:22-25 The fruit of the Spirit is love, joy, peace, longsuffering, gentleness, goodness, faith, meekness, temperance; against which there is no law. And they that are Christ have crucified the flesh with the affections and lusts, and if we live in the Spirit let us walk in the Spirit. (He said) Jer 29:13 and ye shall seek me and find me when you search for me with all your heart. Eph 1:4 accordingly as He hath chosen us in Him before the foundation of the world that we should be holy and without blame before Him in love. (see also Eph 1:5-14)

Is 54:10 for the mountains shall depart, and the hills be removed; but my kindness shall not depart from thee; neither shall the covenant of my peace be removed; saith the Lord that have mercy on thee. 2 Cor 1:20 for all the promises of God in Him are yea and in Him Amen unto the glory of God by us. Luke 24:49 and behold I send the promise of my father upon you, but tarry.............until ye be endured with power from on high. Ps 91:1-2 He that dwelleth in the secret place of the most high shall abide under the shadow of the Almighty. I will say of the Lord; He is my refuge and fortress; my God; in Him will I trust. Matt 10:16 He said, behold I send you forth as sheep in the midst of wolves; be ye therefore wise as serpents and harmless as doves. Is 41:10 Fear thou not, for I am with thee, be not dismayed, for I am thy God, I will strengthen thee, yea, I will help thee; yes I will uphold thee with the right hand is my righteousness. Is 54:17 No weapon formed against thee shall prosper, and every tongue that shall rise against the in judgement thou shall condemn. Ps 91.10 there shall no evil befall thee, neither shall any plague come nigh thy dwelling.

Pray the Lord's Prayer today and to receive your blessings read 1 John 5:1-15. The life you are living or chose to live will speak louder than your lips. For there are three that bear record in heaven, The Father, The Word and the Holy Ghost and these three are One; and there are three that bear witness in earth, the Spirit, the Water and the Blood and these three agree in One. And this is the record that God hath given to us eternal life, and this life Is in His Son. Amen and thank you Jesus.

Having A Relationship With God

Created on 2017-11-19 11:52

Matt 24:35 Heaven and earth will pass away, but my words will by no means pass away. Isa 40:8 The word of our God stands forever. Prov 30:5-8 Every word of God is pure. He is a shield to those who put their trust in Him. Do not add to His words lest He rebuke you, and you be found a liar. Two things I request of you, remove falsehood and lies far from me, feed me with the food allotted to me. Lam 3:22 Through the Lord's mercies we are not consumed because His compassion fail not.

Jesus said, Matt 24:24 False Christs and false prophets will rise and show great signs and wonders to deceive, if possible even the elect. Matt 24:25 See I have told you beforehand.

1 Corin 1:9, God is faithful, by which you were called into the fellowship of His son, Jesus Christ our Lord.

Ps 119:11 Your word I have hidden in my heart that I might not sin against you. Ps 17:8 Keep me as the apple of your eye. Hide me under the shadow of your wings. Ps 91:1 He who dwells in the secret place of the Most High shall abide under the shadow of the Almighty. Ps 40:81 delight to do your will, O my God. And your law is within my heart. Lam 3:58 O Lord you have pleaded the case for my soul; you have redeemed my life.

Jesus said in John 6:40 and this is the will of Him who sent Me, that everyone who sees the Son and believes in Him may have everlasting life and I will raise him up at the last day. Matt 6:30 for the bread of life is He who comes down from heaven and gives life to the world. Matt 6:35 I am the bread of life. He who comes to me shall never hunger, and he who believes in me shall never thirst. John 10:10 the thief does not come except to steal, and to kill and to destroy. I have come that they may have life, and that they may have it more abundantly. John 6:47 Most assuredly, I say to you, he who believes in me has everlasting life. Matt 16:25 whosoever desires to save his life will lose it, but whosoever loses his life for My sake will find it. John 6:48 I am the bread of life. John 10:11 I am the good shepherd. The good shepherd gives His life for the sheep.

John 1:4 In Him was life, and the life was the light of men.

Jer 39:18 For I will surely deliver you, and you shall not fall by the sword; but your life shall be as a prize to you because you have put your trust in me, says the LORD.

Rom 8:2 the law of the Spirit of life in Christ Jesus has made me free from the law of sin and death. John 5:21 for as the Father raised the dead and gives life to them even so the Son gives life to whom He will.

Matt 12:50 whosoever does the will of my Father in heaven is my brother and sister and mother.

1 Cor 13:13 and now abide faith, hope, love; these three, but the greatest is these is love. 2 Gal 5:22-23 But the fruit of the Spirit is love, joy, peace, longsuffering, kindness, goodness, faithfulness, gentleness, self-control. Against such there is no law. 24-25 and those that are Christ's have crucified the flesh with its passions and desires. If we live in the Spirit let us also walk in the Spirit. Col 3:14-15 But above all these things, put on love which is the bond of perfection, and let the peace of God rule in your hearts, to which also you were called in one body and be thankful.

Luke 12:22 Therefore I say to you, do not worry about your life, what you will eat, nor about the body what you will put on. Prov 12:28 in the way of righteousness is life and in the pathway there is no death. Col 3:4 when Christ who is our life appears, then you also shall appear with Him in glory.

Develop a relationship with God today. Start by praying as JESUS taught us how to pray. Pray the Lord's Prayer. Not just today, but everyday.

Set aside time to pray daily to ABBA FATHER. Father please hear my voice as I lift my hands to Thee. Bless all the readers in some small way, in the name of Jesus. Thank you. Amen and Amen.

How We Know Jesus Exist And Why

Created on 2016-12-25 12:27

John 3:16 For God so loved the world, that he gave His only begotten son, that whosoever believeth in Him should not perish, but have everlasting life. Amos 8:11 Behold, the days come, saith the Lord, that I will send a famine to the land, not a famine of bread, not a thirst for water, but of hearing the words of the Lord. Matt 5:6 Blessed are they which do hunger and thirst after righteousness, for they shall be filled. Jesus said in John 4:14 But whosoever drinketh of the water that I give him shall never thirst, but the water I shall give him be in him a well of water springing up into everlasting life. Jesus said in John 8:12 I am the Light of the world, he that follow me shall not walk in darkness, but shall have the Light of Life. John 3:34 For He whom God hath sent speaketh the words of God, for God giveth not the Spirit by measure unto Him. Phil 2:9-10 Wherefore God also hath highly exalted Him and given Him a name which is above every name, that at the name of Jesus, every knee should bow.......Is 7:14 Therefore the Lord Himself shall give you a sign; behold a virgin shall conceive, and bear a son and shall call His name Immanuel.

Jesus had a virgin earthly vessel as his mother and a heavenly Father. Jesus was born in human flesh sent to die for humanity to reconcile humanity back to God. Jesus is the living Word of God. Jesus is the living God who lived before He was conceived. He preexisted with God. How do we know that? In Gen 1:26 God said, Let US make man in OUR image, after OUR likeness.......so God created man in His own image, in the image of God created He him: male and FEMALE created He them. John 1:1-5 In the beginning was the word and the word was with God, and the word was God. The same was in the BEGINNING WITH GOD. ALL things were made by Him and without Him was not anything made that was made. In Him was Life and the Life was the Light of man. And the Light shineth in the darkness; and the darkness comprehended it not. Jesus is the true Light of the world through which all men might believe.

Jesus was born into a world which He created. Colos 1:14-16 (see also 17-22) We have redemption through His blood, even the forgiveness of sin. Jesus power holds everything together. He is the image of the invisible God, the firstborn of every creature. For by Him were all things created, that are in heaven and that are in the earth, visible and invisible, whether they be thrones, or dominions, or principalities, or powers: all things were created by Him and for Him.

Heb 1:1-5 God hath spoken. He hath in these last days spoken unto us by His son, whom He hath appointed heir of all things by whom also He made the worlds, who being the brightness of His glory and the express image of His person and upholding ALL things by the WORD of His power, when He had by Himself purged our sins, sat down on the right hand of the Majesty on high. God did not say to any of the angels at any time "thou art my son, this day have I begotten thee, and again I will be to him a Father and he shall be to me a son."

Jesus said "I and the Father are One. John 10:27-30 Jesus said, "My sheep hear my voice and I know them, and they follow Me. And I give unto them eternal life, they shall never perish neither shall any man pluck them out of my hand. My Father which gave them Me, is greater than ALL. And no man is able to pluck them out of my Father's hand. I and my Father are One. John 12:44-45 Jesus said that he that believeth on Me believe not on Me but on Him that sent Me. I am come a Light into the world, that whosoever believe in Me shall not abide in darkness.

Jesus came in a visible physical form fashioned as a man. The birth of Jesus: remember Luke 2:11-14 the angel of the Lord said for unto you is born this day in the city of David, a Savior; which is Christ the Lord. Luke 2:15 The Lord had made it known unto us. Isa 9:2 The people that walked in darkness have seen a great light: they that dwell in the land of the shadow of death, upon them hath the light shined. Isa 9:16 for unto us a child is born and unto us a child is given and the government shall be upon his shoulder and His name shall be called: Wonderful, Counsellor, The Mighty God, The Everlasting Father, The Prince of Peace. (read vs 7) Isaiah stated the prophecy of Jesus birth. Matthew stated the fulfillment of His birth. Matt 4:16-15 and the people which sat in darkness saw a great light and to them which sat in the region and shadow of death, Light is sprung up.

Ps 16:8 I have set the Lord always before me. Because He is at my right hand, I shall not be moved. Habuk 2:1-2 I will stand upon my watch and set me upon the tower and I will watch and see what He will say unto me, and what I shall answer when I am reproved. And the Lord answered me and said: write the vision and make it plain upon tables that he may run that readeth it. Rev 22:1-5 And He showed me a pure river of water of life, clear as crystal, proceeding out of the throne of God and of the Lamb. In the midst of the street of it, and on either side of the river, was there the tree of life, which bare 12 manner of fruits, and yielded her fruit every month, and the leaves of the tree were for the healing of the nations. And there shall be: but the throne of God and the Lamb shall be in it, and His servants shall serve Him, and they shall see His face, and His name shall be in their foreheads. And there shall be no night there., and they need no candle, neither light of the son, for the Lord God giveth them light; and they shall reign for ever and ever. Acts 26-28 Therefore did my heart rejoice and my tongue was glad,-----Thou will not suffer thine Holy One to see corruption. Thou hast made known to me the ways of life. Thou shall make me full of joy with thy countenance. John 3:16 For God so loved the world, that He gave His only begotten son, that whosoever believeth in Him should not perish, but have everlasting life. Pray the Lord's Prayer today and the 23rd & 100th Psalms.

How I Pray For Favorable Results

Created on 2017-04-08 10:18

I am going to let you know how I pray and get favorable results. I am not including all the bible scripture references, but I will paraphrase what I read in the bible to enable me to pray effectively.

Make your home with God. Ps 91:1 says He that dwell in the secret place of the MOST HIGH shall abide under the shadow of THE ALMIGHTY. Ps 91:10 says There shall no evil befall thee, neither shall any plaque come nigh thy dwelling. Ps 91:11 says For He shall give His angels charge over thee to keep thee in all thy ways.

In John 15:1 Jesus says I am the true vine. 15:3 Now ye are clean through the word I have spoken unto you. 15:4 abide in me and I in you. 15:7 If ye abide in Me and My word abide in you, ye shall ask what you will, and it shall be done unto you. Act 1:8 Jesus said ye shall receive power, after that the Holy Ghost is come upon you and ye shall be witnesses unto me............ unto the uttermost part of the earth.

I read in the Word seek ye first the kingdom of heaven and all things will become available to you and be yours (paraphrased of course). I read also all good things come down from heaven. I read if two of you agree as touching when you ask you shall receive it from the Father who is in heaven. I read you are to believe you will receive it when you ask, and have no doubt whatsoever. I read when you ask for something, ask for it in the name of Jesus.

When I prayed this time, I asked for some power of Jesus to be given to me. I ask that I use it wisely, positively and to help others with it. I am believing it to be done for I asked for it in His name. I am praying to be able to heal others in every way they may need healing: Spiritually, physically, mentally, emotionally, financially (which means I am believing God for a substantial increase financially in my life to be able to help others and the churches in need). Whatever the need may be as long as it's not a carnal need.

I am living my life now by the great and First commandment to love the LORD my God with all my heart, all my mind and all my soul. I am believing Him to dwell in me Spiritually and to fill me with His Power. I am going to love everyone even my enemies, but I DON'T HAVE TO LIKE MY ENEMIES WAYS. I am praying to God for them asking God to change them and asking Him to wash them clean.

I will no longer allow negative words to come from my lips, for words are energy, have power and will manifest when you speak them. Remember, for in the beginning was The Word, and The Word was with God and The Word is God manifested in the flesh as Jesus. With God's Word in us we can create any circumstance or thing, good or bad. For God says in Isaiah I create good and evil. I The Lord do all these things.

I will close now, but I want you to start your days by praying The Lord's Prayer. Ask that He wash you with His Word so you will be clean. Ask that you abide in Him and He in you. Ask that His Word abide in you. Then ask for the power of Jesus be given unto you. Once you receive it, use it wisely and for the good of others. You'll find others will bless you. God bless you for reading this article. Have a good, peaceful, beautiful and positive day and be blessed. In Jesus name. Amen and Amen. Thank you God.

Images Of Man God Created & Adam Begot

Created on 2018-04-11 09:14

In Gen 1:26, God said, let us make man in our image, after out likeness, and let them have dominion over the fish of the sea, and the fowl of the air and over the cattle and over all the earth and over every creeping thing that creepeth on the earth. 27 So God CREATED man in His own image, in the image of God CREATED he him; male and female CREATED he them and God blessed them. Gen 2:8 And the Lord God planted a garden eastward in Eden and there He put the man whom He had formed. 2:7 and the Lord formed man of the dust of the ground and breathe into his nostrils the breath of life; and man became a living soul.

John 4:24 says God is a Spirit; and they that worship Him, must worship Him in Spirit and in Truth. Phil 3:3 When we worship God in the Spirit and rejoice in Christ Jesus (who is the Truth) we have no confidence in the flesh. John 14:6 Jesus said, I am the way, the Truth and the life; no man cometh unto the Father but by Me. I (phyllis) ask you to pursue TRUTH. 4:24 The Father seeketh such to worship Him. This led me to believe we were living spirits, living souls when we were first created, in the image and likeness of God who is a spirit. It may be possible man was transformed when Adam and Eve ate of the tree they were forbidden to eat from In Gen 3:22 God said the man is become as one of us to know good and evil which they had not known before they ate of the tree.

Adam's genealogy-Gen 5:1-3 In the day that God created man-in the likeness of God made He him; male and female created He them and blessed them and called their name Adam. After they sinned, a transformation might have occurred for they hid and covered themselves with fig leaves. Adam lived 130 years and BEGAT a son IN HIS OWN LIKENESS AFTER HIS OWN IMAGE and called his name Seth. Maybe that is why it is written in the bible ye must be born again, to have power to become the sons of God even to them that believe on His name which were born not of blood, nor of the will of the flesh, nor of the will of man, but of God. John 1:13

Beloved, you must be born again -get baptized by water and then baptized by the Holy Spirit. In John 3:3 Jesus said verily verily I say unto thee, except a man be born again, he cannot see the kingdom of God. Verily verily I say unto thee except a man be born of the water and the Spirit, he can not enter into the kingdom of God, that which is born of the flesh is flesh (which is what Seth was when he was born of Adam) and that which is born of the Spirit is spirit (which is what Adam was before he sinned when God CREATED him). vs 8 Jesus said the wind bloweth where it listeth and thou hearest the sound thereof, but cannot tell whence it cometh or whither it goeth, so is everyone that is born of the Spirit. 12 I have told you earthly things and you believed not, how shall ye believe when I tell you of heavenly things.

13 No man ascended up to heaven but He that came down even the Son of man which is in heaven...........14 even so must the Son of man be lifted up that whosoever believeth in Him should not perish but have eternal life. 16 For God so loved the world that he gave HIS only begotten son, that whosoever believeth in Him should not perish but have everlasting life. 18 he that believeth on Him is not condemned. Read 1 Corin 15:51-58 51behold, I show you a mystery; we shall not all sleep but we all shall be changed. 53 Corruptible must put on incorruption and mortal must put on immortality.

1 Corin 15:45-47 and so it is written the 1st man Adam was made a living soul; the last Adam was made a quickening Spirit. The 1st man is of the earth, earthy. The second man is the LORD from heaven. 49 and as we hath borne the image of the earthy, we shall also bear the image of the heavenly. 50 Flesh and blood cannot inherit the kingdom of God. 51 behold I show you a mystery; we shall not all sleep but we all shall be

changed, he sown a natural body it is raised a spiritual body. There is a natural body and a spiritual body. 54 death is swallowed up in victory. 57 but thanks be to God, which giveth us the victory through our Lord Jesus Christ..John 10:34 Jesus said is it not written in your laws I said ye are gods? Ps 82:6 I have said ye are gods, and all of you are children of the most high...7 but ye shall die like men..............

Rev 7:13-17..........What are these which are arrayed in white robes? and hence came they? and I said unto him, sir, thou knowest, and he said to me these are they which came out of great tribulation and have washed their robes and made them white in the blood of the Lamb therefore are they before the throne of God and serve Him day and night in His temple and He that sitteth on the throne shall dwell among them. They shall hunger no more neither thirst any more neither shall the sun light on them nor any heat. For the Lamb which is in the midst of the throne shall feed them and shall lead them unto living fountains of water, and God shall wipe away all tears from their eyes...

I don't know who said it but Faith is seeing light with your heart when all your eyes see is darkness. Pray the Lord's Prayer today, and the 23rd, 100, & 125 Psalms Read the 119 and 91st Psalms. Hotep!!! You awaken this morning. Now take time out to thank the Divine power for allowing you to continue to breath the breath He put within you. Think, act, be and communicate in a positive way today. Project LOVE. I leave you now as I came to you in peace and love. Hotep!!!

Instructions To
The People

Created on 2016-06-17 9:31

Ps 29:11 The Lord will give strength unto His people; the Lord will bless His people with peace. Rev 21:6 It is done. I AM Alpha and Omega, the beginning and the end; I will give unto him that is athirst of the fountain of the water of life freely. John 14:27 Peace, I leave with you, my peace I give unto you; not as the world giveth, give I unto you. Let not your heart be troubled, neither let it be afraid. Phil 11:9 Those things, which ye have both learned and received and heard and seen in me, do: and the God of peace shall be with you.

Eph 5:17, 20 Wherefore be ye not unwise, but understanding what the will of the Lord is. Giving thanks always for all things unto God and the Father in the name of our Lord Jesus Christ. John 15:7 If ye abide in me and my word abide in you, ye shall ask what ye will, and it shall be done unto you. John 16:23-24 Whatsoever ye shall ask the Father in my name, He will give it you. In my name, ask, and you may receive, that your joy may be full. Mark 11:23 Do not doubt in your heart, believe and it shall come to pass, you shall have whatever. Prov 23:26 My son, give me thine heart, and let thine eyes observe my ways.

2 Chron 7:14 If my people which are called by my name, shall humble themselves, and pray and seek my face, and turn from their wicked ways, then I will hear from heaven, and will forgive their sin, and will heal their land. Josh 1:8-9 This book of the law shall not depart out of thy mouth, but thou

shalt meditate therein day and night, that thou mayest observe to do according to all that is written therein, for then thou shalt make thy way prosperous, and then thou shall have good success. Have not I commanded thee? Be not afraid neither be thou dismayed; for the Lord thy God is with thee whithersoever thou goest.

It's Scamming Time Again

Created on 2020-12-12 12:59

It's that time again where scamming elderly people is more prevalent. I will tell you of my situation. I applied for three loans. Two financial institutions deposited the money into my account without asking me to apply for an on-line banking account. The third financial institution had me apply for and open an on-line banking account, and give them access to it for them to deposit my loan amount into it. Thinking nothing wrong, I gave them access to the account. Then I remembered what I did with the other two institutions was to give them a cancelled check. **NOW HERE IS THE SCAM.** They deposit a check into your account. The bank makes part of the money available. The loan company contact you and tell you to send the money the bank made available to them because it was their money to make a test deposit to verify who you were. They will tell you to send a money gram or a google play card for the amount made available. After you do that they will deposit your loan amount into your account. Of course you will have to send back the balance of the 1st deposit made into your account. I am telling you **UNDER NO CIRCUMSTANCES SHOULD YOU TOUCH THE MONEY WHICH BECAME AVAILABLE.** They put so much pressure on me to send it. They even threatened to take legal action against my social security. But here is the thing-I **NEVER SIGNED A CONTRACT FOR THE LOAN,** they knew this and deposited money into my bank account anyway, and said they would deposit the $5000 into my account after I sent them the $200 which became available. I told them I no longer wanted the loan. They sent me two threats to my cell phone. I contacted the bank and asked them to close my account after I explained what I had experienced. The bank investigated the deposit transaction and told me the check they deposited was fake. They put a hold on my account and will take further action. They told me not to answer any more contacts from the loan company. The key thing I wish to point out to you is under no circumstances should you touch a deposit made available to you because you are being scammed if you do and you will end up owing the bank. This is a holiday season. Be alert to the possibility of plenty of different scams being played on you. Hotep!!! I go in peace and hope this info was helpful to you. Again, Peace.

by phyllis b. ames-bey

Is The Christianity
You Are Believing In
False Christianity

Created on 2015 07/04 09:14

Check out the meat being served. John 17:17 Sanctify them through thy truth, thy word is truth. Beware of those who talk about Jesus and the Bible, but are not delivering the message of Christ. They should preach about the Gospel of God which is about the Grace of God. If anyone preach any other gospel other than about the Grace of God, they are accursed. Paul said to preach about the Grace of God in Romans 1:15, Galatians 1:6-9 and Acts 20:24. His grace is sufficient for me. Beware of Satan tactics. As per Revelations 12:9-11, he deceives the whole world. We will get to that after this message.

1 Peter 5:5-8 likewise, ye younger, submit yourselves unto the elder. Yea, all of you be subject one to another; and be clothed with humility; for God resisted the proud, and giveth grace to the humble. Humble yourselves therefore under the mighty hand of God, that he may exalt you in due time. Casting all your care upon him, for he careth for you. Be sober, be vigilant, because your adversary the devil, as a roaring lion, walketh about, seeking whom he may devour.

Rev 12:9-11 and the great dragon was cast out, that old serpent, called the devil, and satan, which deceiveth the whole world; he was cast out into the earth, and his angels were cast out with him. And I heard a loud voice saying in heaven, Now is come salvation, and strength, and the Kingdom of our God, and the power of his Christ: for the accuser of our brothern is cast down, which accused them before our God day and night. And they overcame them by the blood of the Lamb, and by the word of their testimony, and they loved not their lives unto death.

Rev 2:7 & 9 He that hath an ear, let him hear what the spirit saith unto the churches; to him that overcometh will I give to eat of the tree of life, which is in the midst of the paradise of God. I know thy works, and tribulations, and poverty and I know the blasphemy of them which say they are Jews, and are not, but are the synagogue of satan. Fear none of those things which thou shalt suffer, behold the devil shall cast some of you into prison, they ye may be tried, and ye shall have tribulation ten days; be thou faithful unto death, and I will give thee a crown of life. 1 Corin 16:9 For a great door and effectual is opened unto me, and there are many adversaries.

Matt 15:13-14 Every plant, which my Heavenly Father hath not planted shall be rooted up. Let them alone: they be blind leaders of the blind, and if the blind lead the blind, both shall fall into the ditch. 2 Corin 11:13-15 For such are false apostles, deceitful workers, transforming themselves into the apostles of Christ, and no marvel; for satan himself is transformed into an angel of light. Therefore it is no great thing if his ministers also be transformed as the ministers of righteousness; whose end shall be according to their works. Isaiah 8:20 to the law and to the testimony; if they speak not according to the word, it is because there is no light in them.

Matt 7:13-16 Enter ye in at the strait gate: for wide is the gate, and broad is the way, that leadeth to destruction, and many there be which go in thereat; because strait is the gate, and narrow is the way, which leadeth unto life, and few there be that find it. Beware of false prophets, which come to you in sheep's clothing, but inwardly they are ravening wolves. Ye shall know them by their fruits. 2 Chron 11:4 thus said the Lord, ye shall not go up, nor fight against your brethren, return every man to his house; for this thing is done of me, and they obeyed the word of the Lord.

2 Chron 18:18-22 Therefore hear the word of the Lord: I saw the Lord sitting upon his throne, and all the host of heaven standing on his right hand and on

his left, and the Lord said, who shall entice Ahab, king of Israel that he may go up and fall at Ramothgilead? and one spake saying after this manner, and another saying after that manner. Then came out a spirit, and stood before the Lord and said, I will entice him and the Lord said unto him. Wherewith? and he said, I will go out, and be a lying spirit in the mouth of all the prophets, and the Lord said, thou shall entice him, and thou shall also prevail; go out and do even so. Now, therefore, behold, the Lord hath put a lying spirit in the mouth of those thy prophets, and the Lord hath spoken evil against thee.

Ephes6:10-19 Be strong in the Lord and the power of his might; put on the whole armour of God that ye may be able to stand against the wiles of the devil. For we wrestle not against flesh and blood but against the principalities, against powers, against the rulers of darkness of this world, against spiritual wickedness in high places. Wherefore take unto you the whole armour of God, that ye may be able to withstand in the evil day, and having done all to stand. Stand therefore having your loins girt about with truth, and having on the breastplate of righteousness and your feet shod with the preparation of the gospel of peace, above all taking the shield of faith, wherewith ye shall be able to face the fiery darts, of the wicked, and take the helmet of salvation and the sword of the spirit, which is the word of God, praying always with all prayer and supplication in the spirit, and watching there unto with all perseverance and supplication for all saints, and for me, that utterance may be given unto me, that I may open my mouth boldly to make known the mystery of the gospel...

Ephes1:9 Having made known to us the mystery of his will, according to his good pleasure which he hath proposed in himself: that in the dispensation of the fullness of times, He might gather together in one all things in Christ, both which are in heaven and which are on earth even in him. In whom also we have an inheritance, being predestimated according to the purpose of him who worketh all things after the counsel of his own will that we should be to the praise of his glory, who first trusted in Christ.

Ephes1:16 Cease not to give thanks Ephes1:17-18 that the God of our Lord Jesus Christ, the Father of glory, may give unto you the spirit of wisdom and revelation in the knowledge of him: The eyes of your understanding being enlightened, that ye may know what is the hope of his calling and what the riches of the glory of his inheritance in the saints.

Please, please continue in your reading of Ephesians 1:19-23 for the rest of the revelation and knowledge.

Also read 2 Thess2:1-17. This concludes my first and only post about the word of God, the meat, the Holy Ghost Spirit anointed me to share with you. AMEN

Is There More Than
Two Comings Of Jesus

Created on 201???-03-18 12:41

Whose got the victory with you, JESUS or satan? Jesus won the battle between Him and satan when He was at His weakest moment after fasting 40 days by telling satan 3 words, it is written, three times. He went to hell and took the keys of death. He won the battle again when He was resurrected. He won the battle again in saving souls. When YOU come against the devil again and he start whispering something in your ear which is contrary to your belief, honesty and integrity, rebuke him by allowing the Spirit of Jesus which dwell in you say, get thee behind me satan for it is written in God's word if I resist the devil, he will flee from me. Tell satan to take his hands off of you, your home, your family, your health, your finances and stop fighting your Spirit in Jesus name. Loose the law of abundance over your life. See Matt 18:18 whatsoever ye shall bind on earth shall be bound in heaven; and whatsoever ye shall loose on earth shall be loose in heaven.

Are there more than two comings of Jesus? I believe the birth of Jesus was the first coming, foretold in Isaiah 6:10, 14-16. The LORD spake again unto Ahaz, saying, Therefore the Lord Himself shall give you a sign; behold a virgin shall conceive and bear a son, and shall call His name Immanuel. Butter and honey shall He eat, that He may know to refuse the evil, and choose the good. Matt 1:21-23 And she shall bring forth a son that THOU shall call His name JESUS; for He shall save His people from sin. Now all this was done, that it might be fulfilled which was spoken of the LORD by the prophet saying behold, a virgin shall be with child and shall bring forth a son and they shall call His name Emmanuel, which being interpreted is, GOD with us.

There will come a day when prophets should not prophesy for in Zec 13:2-9 the Lord said I will cut off the names of the idols out of the land and I will cause the prophets and unclean spirits to pass out of the land. And it shall come to pass that when any shall yet prophesy, then his father and mother shall say unto him, thou shall not live for thou speaketh lies in the name of the Lord. And it shall come to pass in that day he shall say, I am no prophet. I am a husbandman, for man taught me to keep cattle from my youth. And one shall say unto him, what are these wounds in thine hands? Then he shall answer, these which which I was wounded in the house of my friends.

Awake o sword, against my shepherd and against the man that is my fellow, saith the Lord of hosts: smite the shepherd and the sheep will be scattered and I will turn mine hand upon the little ones. And it shall come to pass, that in all the land, saith the lord, two parts therein shall be cut off and die, and the third part shall be left therein. And I will bring the third part through the fire, and will refine them as silver and I will try them as gold is tried, they shall call on my name, and I will hear them; I will say it is my people, and they shall say, the Lord is my God. The Lord will be king over all the earth. For there will be a battle in which the Lord will have the victory. In that day there shall be one Lord and His name one. See Zec. chapter 14.

Getting back to the coming of JESUS. In Matthew chapter 27 Jesus is crucified. In Matthew Chapter 28, He came back to life-He is risen from the dead. (Was that His second coming?) for in verse 18-20 Jesus said all power is given unto me in heaven and in earth. Go ye therefore and teach all nations, baptizing in the name of the Father and the Son and the Holy Ghost: teaching them to observe all things whatsoever I have command you, and lo, I am with you always, even until the end of the world. Amen. See also the great commission in Mark 16:15-20, Luke 24:36-53 and John 20:17-23. John 20:30-31 many things were not written that Jesus had done but these things are written that ye might know Jesus is the Christ, the Son of God, and that believing ye might have life through His name.

Is what is written in Revelation actually His third coming? In Rev 1:8 He says, I am Alpha and Omega, the beginning and the ending which Is, which Was AND which Is To Come, THE ALMIGHTY, verses 17-18 Fear not; I am the first and the last; I am He the liveth and was dead and behold I am alive forever more, Amen; and have the keys of hell and of death. In Rev 22:7 Behold I come quickly; blessed is he that keep the sayings of the prophesy of this book, (food that is my thought-is He referring to the Bible, the Torah or the book of Revelation? For I believe He taught from the Torah but He is also the covenant between us, Him, the Father and the Holy Ghost. I understand this as what is written in the New Testament and in Isaiah of the old testament. This causes me to believe He is referring to the ENTIRE Bible). See Rev 22:12-13 and 16 & 20.

Is when we die, we actually experience the coming He speaks of. Two thirds will be rejected and one third will be saved. Are the people who become cremated His people being tried by fire spoken of in Isaiah and Revelation? I am searching for knowledge and understanding for He provided us the truth for us to gain knowledge of it. For in Rev 19:11-21, it speaks of a great war between God and satan. Chapter 20 v 14-15 speaks of the SECOND death and those not found written in the book of life was cast into the lake of fire. Rev 21 speaks of the new heaven and earth and the New Jerusalem coming down from God out of heaven. And Jesus said IT IS DONE. Pray the Lord's Prayer today and I will continue searching scripture to find answers, gain knowledge, understanding and wisdom.

Jesus Spirit Did Not Die When He Died On The Cross

Created on 2016-06-08 11:18

ABBA FATHER, as I commune with my heart, I realize I am a sinner trying to live as a saint. But that is not a bad thing for you bore all my sins when your body died on the cross. I will try harder to stop sinning. I think people have not thought of nor realized though the son of Mary's body died, your Spirit did not die for you put your Spirit into the hands of God the Father. Then your Spirit went to hell, defeated satan and death and you took the keys of Hades and Death as per Revelation 1:18.

You also had some other keys for in your word Matthew 16:19 you stated you would give us the keys of the kingdom of heaven and whatever we bind on earth will be bound in heaven also whatever we loose on earth will be loosed in heaven. Revelation 3:7 says you have the keys of David. You opens and no one shuts, you shuts and no one opens.

I just realized with the Holy Ghost Spirit dwelling within me I can be super human. I can do all things through Christ. We can call those things that be not as though they were. I am not claiming to be perfect Lord Jesus, because you are the only one who is perfect. I just have a perfect Spirit dwelling in an imperfect body.

Lord Jesus I want to end this prayer by telling your people to remember to pray the Lords Prayer daily and for those who are living in fear of their enemies to pray the 35 Psalm verses 1-9. Turn it over to you and your angels, for the battle is not theirs. Prayer is very effective. I am also asking them to clean themselves up. Break the addiction to drugs, alcohol and smoking because they are things of the world and belong to satan. Allow the Holy Ghost Spirit to dwell in a clean temple. We have been redeemed and there is no condemnation in Christ. I thank you Father for hearing my prayer and allowing me to share it with others. Amen and Amen.

Living in the Body
Of Christ

Created on 2017-06-21 15:58

I welcome those of you coming in Spirit and in Truth. Is45:22 Look unto Me and be ye saved, all the ends of the earth, for I AM GOD, and there is none else. Is 45:18-19 Thus said the Lord that created the heavens: God Himself that formed the earth and made it; He hath established it. He created it not in vain. He formed it to be inhabited; I AM THE LORD and there is none else. I have not spoken in secret, in a dark place of the earth; I said not unto the seed of Jacob seek ye Me in vain; I the Lord speak righteousness, I declare things that are right. Is45:23 I have sworn by Myself, the Word is gone out of my mouth in righteousness, and shall not return, that unto Me every knee shall bow, every tongue shall swear.

Ps84:11 For the Lord God is a Sun and a Shield. The Lord will give grace and glory, no good thing will He withhold from them that walk uprightly. Humble yourselves in the sight of the Lord and He shall lift you up. 4:11 speak not evil of another. 4:17to him that knoweth to do good, and doeth it not, to him it is sin. Rom8:5 For they that are after the flesh do mind the things of the flesh, but they that are after the Spirit the things of the Spirit.

Eph2:8 For by grace are ye saved through faith, and that not of yourselves; it is the gift of God. Eph2:10 For we are His workmanship, created in Christ Jesus unto good works, which God hath before ordained that we would walk in them. 2nd Corin5:17 Therefore if any man be in Christ, he is a new creature; old things are passed away; behold, all things are become new. Gal

5:22-23 The fruit of the Spirit is love, joy, peace, longsuffering, gentleness, goodness, faith, meekness, temperance; against such there is no law.24 and they that are Christ's have sacrificed the flesh with the affections and lust. 25 If we live in the Spirit let us also walk in the Spirit.

Lam 3:22 It is of the Lord's mercies that we are not consumed, because His compassions fail not. 23 They are new every morning, great is thy faithfulness. 25 The Lord is good unto those that wait for Him, to the soul that seeketh Him. 26 It is good that a man should both hope and quietly wait for the salvation of the Lord. 31 For the Lord will not cast off forever. 32 But though He cause grief, yet will He have compassion according to the multitude of His mercies. 33 For He does not afflict willingly nor grieve the children of men. 40 Let us search and try our ways and turn again to the lord. Now let us pray the Lord's Prayer and give thanks to Jesus. Amen and Amen.

My Experience With Wod Magazine

Created on 2017-01-17 19:42

In 2015, I was solicited by Women of Distinction to have an article published in their magazine. The original price was $375 to get my story told. Later, they called and stated I had been selected for the cover of October 2015 issue. They gave me updated information saying it was too late to be placed on October so I would be on November 2015 issue. When the magazines were printed, they gave me copies of both months. The one for October featured the article. The one for November featured me on the cover and the article on the first few pages of the magazine. Of course, I had to pay additional money for being on the cover.

Women of Distinction Magazine contacted me again in 2016 stating their Honors Department was looking forward to featuring me and my article again. I would now be noted as Recipient of the 2016 Excellence Award. I would be receiving two plaques, however, I must pay $595 for them. I paid the money to them with a credit card on 2/29/16. In April, I was contacted by them again with the offer of being featured on the cover of October 2016 magazine as the recipient of the 2016 Excellence Award along with my article. I stated I would like to update my article first. On Thursday May 26, 2016 I received a copy of the final draft of how my article would appear in the magazine.

I am getting ahead of myself. When they contacted me about October's issuance they advised me it would cost $1000, then they dropped the price down to $750. I gave them my credit card number-a different one-for payment. They advised me after the fact that I would see on my statement Bloomgarden, Goudreft Lauderdaleft took the money off of my card and identified them as their lawyers. I did not give my permission for that to happen. They took the money off of my card 5/3/16.

I wrote and called them several times by e-mail and phone regarding the two plaques and the article and the magazine cover. No one is responding. All phone calls and letters were ignored. It is even set up if I call any of their phone numbers from either of my phones. I am unable to speak with anyone and also is not able to have access to any employee's mailbox. I had no recourse but to file a complaint with the Attorney General Bureau of Consumer Protection.

I advised them I paid Women of Distinction for services which should have been rendered by October 2016, but as of this date 01/17/17 the services remain unfilled. I advised them of everything I am sharing with you in the above sequence. I enclosed all types of documentation to them: credit card statements, a copy of the final article and acknowledge of receipt of same, names of who I contacted, all emails sent, I also have if they need it, a recorded voice mail message from their employee backing up my complaint about them advising me their lawyer took the money from my card.

I close this article by advising you if you have experienced or is currently experiencing not receiving goods or services you paid for from a solicitor or company etc. either get a lawyer, contact the Better Business Bureau or file a complaint with the Attorney General of the Consumer Protection Agency, or file a claim in Small Claims Court. Have plenty of documentation to back up your complaint and hope the dispute gets settled in your favor. In addition, start checking things out before you get involved by investigating, or googling, or checking Better Business Bureau to find out if there are any existing complaints. Learn from my experience.

Obedience To God

Created on 2017-02-27 12:00

Are you hardhearted like Pharaoh who said in Exodus 5:2 who is the LORD, that I should obey His voice and also said I do not know the LORD. Deut11:26-27 the Lord said, Behold, I set before you this day a blessing and a curse: a blessing if ye obey the commandments of the Lord your God which I command you this day and a curse, if ye will not obey the commandment of the Lord your God, but turn aside out of the way which I command you this day, to go after other gods, which ye have not known.

Job 36:11-12 says if they obey and serve Him; they shall spend their days in prosperity and their years in pleasure; if they do not-they shall perish by the sword, and they shall die without knowledge. It appears the world refuses to be taught. God said, this thing command I them, saying, obey my voice, and I will be your God, and ye shall be my people, and walk ye in all the ways that I have commanded you. See also Jeremiah 11:1-4 in which god spoke of a covenant, and told the people, obey MY voice, according to all which I command you, so shall ye be my people and I will be your God.

In Matt 8:27 the winds and the sea obeyed JESUS. In Mark 1:27 the uncleaned spirits obeyed JESUS. Eph 6:1 says children obey your parents in the LORD, for this is right. See also Josh 24:24:22, Acts 5:29 obey God rather than men, Rom 6:16 his servants ye are to whom ye obey, 2 Thes 1:8 Heb 13:17 1 Pet 1:22, Ex 5:2, Ex 22:21 and Dan 9:10. All these scriptures are about obedience to GOD. I ran across a song called Trust and Obey. Here are the words: The song was written by John H. Sammis.

When we walk with the Lord in the light of His Word, What a glory He sheds on our way! While we do His good will, He abides with us still, and with all who will trust and obey. Refrain: Trust and obey for there's no other way to be happy in Jesus, but to trust and obey.

Not a shadow can rise, not a cloud in the skies, but His smile quickly drives it away; not a doubt or a fear, not a sigh or a tear, can abide while we trust and obey.

Not a burden we bear, not a sorrow we share, but our toil He does richly repay; not a grief or a loss, not a frown or a cross but is blessed if we trust and obey.

But we never can prove the delights of His love until all on the altar we lay; for the favor He shows, for the joy He bestows, are for them who will trust and obey.

Then in fellowship sweet we will sit at His feet, or we'll walk by His side in the way; what He says we will do, where He sends we will go; never fear only trust and obey. Trust and obey, for there's no other way to be happy in Jesus, but to trust and obey.

PRAY THE LORD'S PRAYER TODAY. BE BLESSED.

Raped, Abused, Tortured-What Would You Do?

Created on 2016-07-10 12;28

What would you do if someone raped, abused, tortured and terrorized you, your mother, grandmother, daughter, sister, aunt, male relative or other relative of yours? Just what do you do? One may have been sodomized, burned with a cigarette or cigar, cut with a razor of knife, strangled, suffocated, or other horror by the abuser. What would you do? Examine yourself. Remember JESUS suffered before His body died. They beat Him until His meat hung in strips down His back. They pierced Him in the side. The nailed His hands and feet. He forgave them fully, freely and finally.

Eph 4:31-32 says let all bitterness, and wrath and anger and clamour and evil speaking be put away from you with all malice; and be ye kind one to another, forgiving one another, even as God for Christ sake hath forgiven you. We ask God to forgive our trespass as we forgive those who trespass against us. God said to forgive them for what was done as He forgave what was done to Him. Why does God allow bad things to happen to good people? Look and read the book of JOB. The enemy came to kill and destroy.

How do you fight the enemy? You are normally attacked at the point of your weakness. You suffer physically, mentally, emotionally, financially and Spiritually. But you suffered because of what was in the spirit of that person. Do not run and do not fight them on their territory. Remember we are living in spiritual warfare and fighting powers of darkness. What matters to them is what they want to do. You pick the territory or someplace you are familiar with and take the fight to them, if you must fight.

We are just and live by faith so we can take possession of all God has given to us or what God has already done for us. Be responsible. Do not resort to situations quickly. Think about how Jesus would respond. Remember how He reacted to the people who were gambling in the temple.

I speak about this from experiencing the hurt, pain and suffering. I chose to forgive Now I must forget, for I will not put a limit on what God do or can do for me in my life, for I know God favors me. I am maturing gracefully. My body is finally catching up with my spirit because my mind is being renewed. There is power in knowing things, and if you understand and try to do things Christ-like, you will succeed. Hebrews 11:1 says faith is the substance of things hoped for, the evidence of things not seen. What should we hope for? 1 Peter 1:7 that the trial of your faith, being much more precious than gold that perished, though it be tried with fire, might be found unto praise and honor and glory at the appearing of Jesus Christ: Your faith is being put on trial especially when the enemy attacks you and try to destroy you. Just remember, decree claim and believe Isaiah 54:17 no weapon formed against you shall prosper.

Do not let your relationship with God be seriously damaged. We have the power to change our lives That power came from God to us. Hide God's Word in your heart and He will strengthen you. Avoid un-godly things, people and council as it was written, It was written also bad company corrupts good morals. 1 Corinthians 15:33 says be not deceived; evil communications corrupt good manners. Get around people who strengthens you and your walk with God. Gather with the people of God. We are all members of the same body, see 1 Corinthians 12:6 We are submissive and accountable to each other in the body of Christ. Continue to have faith. By grace, we are saved through faith and that not of ourselves, it is the gift of God: Ephesians 2:8 Please end this reading by praying THE LORD'S PRAYER. This I ask in the name of Jesus. AMEN.

Resurrection Sunday
Verses Easter Sunday

Created on 2021-03-30 13:59

I used to celebrate Easter until I learned better. Now I recognize it as Resurrection Sunday. The word Easter is a pagan word. No where in the Bible will you find them celebrating Easter as a day when the Easter bunny come and bring Easter baskets with jelly beans and candy, having a egg hunt, playing with those little yellow chicks until they died. Again, I will say April 4th is Resurrection Sunday.

As per 1 Peter 3:18 Christ also suffered once for sins, the righteous for the unrighteous, that He might bring us to GOD, being put to death in the flesh but made alive in the SPIRIT. 1 Corin 1:23 we preach Christ crucified, a stumbling block to Jew and a folly to Gentiles. Acts 5:30 The GOD of our fathers raised Jesus, whom you killed on a tree. What we should be doing as per Acts 28:31 is proclaiming the Kingdom Of GOD and teaching about the Lord Jesus Christ with all boldness and without hindrance. As per 1 Corin2:13 We should impart this in words not taught by human wisdom but taught by the SPIRIT, interpreting Spiritual Truths to those who are Spiritual. John 20:32 states these are written so that you may believe that JESUS is The Christ, the Son of GOD, and that by believing you may have life in His name.

Col 4:6 Let your speech always be gracious, seasoned with salt, so that you may know how you are to answer each person. Mark 16:15 say go into all the world and proclaim the gospel to the whole creation. Matt 10:7 proclaim as you go saying, "The Kingdom of Heaven is at hand." Mark 1:5 says The time is fulfilled, and the Kingdom of GOD is at hand, repent and believe in the gospel 2 Tim 4:2 Preach the Word: be ready in season and out of season: reprove, rebuke, and exhort with complete patience and teaching. 1 Cor 9:14 In the same way, the LORD commanded that those who proclaim the gospel should get their living by the gospel. Matt 6:33 but seek ye first the Kingdom of God and His righteousness and all these things will be added to you.

1 Tim 4:13 until I come, devote yourself to the public reading of Scripture, to exhortation, to teaching. Read Titus 2 wherein you fill find but as for you, teach what accords with sound doctrine. Older men are to be sober-minded, dignified, self-controlled, sound in faith, in love and in steadfastness. Older women likewise are to be reverent in behavior, not slanderers or slaves to much wine. They are to teach what is good, and so train the young women to love their husbands and children, to be self controlled, pure, working at home, kind, and submissive to their OWN husbands, so that the Word of God will not be reviled...

John 3:16 For GOD so loved the world, that he gave His only Son, that whoever believes in Him should not perish but have eternal life. 1 Cor 15:1-4 Now I would remind you, brothers, of the gospel I preach to you, which you received, in which you stand, and by which you are saved, if you hold fast to the Word I preach to you, unless you believed in vain. For I delivered to you as of first importance what I also received: that Christ died for our sins in accordance with the Scriptures, that He was buried, that He raised on the third day in accordance with the Scriptures.

Gal 3:26 In Christ Jesus you are all sons of GOD, through FAITH. Matt 4:17 From the time Jesus began to preach, saying, repent for the Kingdom of Heaven is at hand. Matt 24:14 And this gospel of the Kingdom will be proclaimed throughout the whole world as a testimony to all nations, and then the end will come, quote-unquote.

Do not be as the false prophets, deceitful workers transforming themselves into the Apostles of Christ. Do not teach god spells instead of gospel, see Luke 24:46-47 Pray, as JESUS taught His disciples to pray---The Lord's Prayer. Please pray it today and every day.

Salvation-A Clear Presentation Of The Gospel On It

Created on 2016-07-14 09:37

The only way of salvation is through JESUS. John 3:16 For God so loved the world, that He gave his only begotten Son, that whosoever believeth in him should not perish, but have everlasting life. John 14:6 JESUS said unto him, I am the way, the truth, and the life: no man cometh unto the Father, but by me. Romans 5:8 But God commended His love toward us, in that, while we were yet sinners, Christ died for us. Ephesians 2:8-9 For by grace are ye saved through faith, and that not of yourselves: it is the gift of God: Not of works, lest any man should boast. Romans 10:9 ...if thou shall confess with thy mouth the Lord Jesus, and shall believe in thine heart that God hath raised him from the dead, thou shalt be saved. Romans 10:13 For whosoever shall call upon the name of the Lord shall be saved. 1 John 1:9 If we confess our sins, he is faithful and just to forgive us our sins, and to cleanse us from all unrighteousness.

JESUS is the only way of salvation. Acts 4:12 Neither is there salvation in any other: for there is none other name under heaven given among men, whereby we must be saved. 1 Timothy 2:5 For there is one God, and one mediator between God and men, the man Christ Jesus. John 3:36 He that believeth on the Son hath everlasting life; and he that believeth not on the Son shall not see life; but the wrath of God abideth on him. John 8:24 I said therefore unto you, that ye shall die in your sins: for if ye believe not that I am He, ye shall die in your sins. John 10:1 Verily, verily, I say unto you, he that entereth not by the door into the sheepfold, but climbeth us some other way, the same is a thief and a robber. John 0:9 I am the door, by Me if any man enter in, he shall be saved, and shall go in and out, and find pasture. John 14:6 JESUS saith unto him, I am the way, the truth and the life, no man cometh unto the Father, but by Me. 1 Corinthians 3:11 for other foundation can no man lay than that is laid, which is Jesus Christ. 1 John 5:12 He that hath the Son hath life, an he that hath not the Son of God hath not life.

On JESUS we should believe. John 3:16 for God so loved the world, that He gave His only begotten Son, that whosoever believeth in Him should not perish, but have everlasting life. John 1:25-26 JESUS said unto her, I am the resurrection, and the life: he that believeth in me, though he were dead, yet shall he live. Believeth thou this? Acts 16:31 and they said, Believe on the Lord Jesus Christ, and thou shalt be saved, and thy house. Romans 10:9-10.....if thou shall confess with thine mouth the Lord Jesus, and shall believe in thine heart that God hath raised Him from the dead, thou shall be saved, for with the heart man believeth unto righteousness; and with the mouth confession is made unto salvation. 1 John 5:1 Whosoever believeth that JESUS is the Christ is born of God: and every one that loveth Him that begat loveth Him also that is begotten of Him.

For salvation, you must receive JESUS, for He said Revelation 3:20 Behold, I stand at the door, and knock: if any man hear my voice, and open the door, I will come in: 12 But as many as received Him, to them gave he power to become the sons of God, even to them that believed on His name. Galatians 4:6 and because eye are sons, God hath sent forth the Spirit of His Son into your hearts, crying, ABBA FATHER, Ephesians 3:17 that Christ may dwell in your hearts by faith; that ye, being rooted and grounded in love.

The scriptures above are being shared with you from two articles I read. The entire readings gave me a clearer picture on what I must do to be saved, and since it did, I am sharing a small portion of what I read with hopes you will have a clearer understanding of salvation and how to obtain it. I feel I am being prepared to become a missionary worker, especially since I was involved in social service work as my profession from 1976 to 2007. It's only right that I use my skills of planning, organizing, directing and overseeing doing work for JESUS.

Scriptures In Honor
Of Mother's Day

Created on 2016-05-07 09:30

Though a woman may give birth to a child, not all of them give the nurturing or love that a true mother does. Some drop their babies down the stool before they are even born. Some abuse their child(ren) or worst. Those women do not deserve to be called mothers. In honor of Mother's Day, let's find out what the WORD has to say about the positive mothers.

Gen 3:20 Adam called his wife's name Eve, because she was the mother of all living. Ex 20:12 Honor thy father and thy mother, that thy days may be long upon the land which the lord thy God giveth thee. Ex 21:15 He that smiteth his father or his mother, shall be surely put to death. Ex 21:17 He that curseth his father or mother, shall surely be put to death. Lev 18:7 The nakedness of thy father's wife, shalt thou not uncover it, it is thy father's nakedness. Lev 20:14 If a man take a wife an her mother, it is wickedness, they shall be burnt with fire.

Now a more positive note-In the book of Ruth, Naomi tried to send her daughter-in-laws away. But they loved her deeply. Ru 1:14 Orpah kissed her mother-in-law but Ruth claved to her. Ru 1:16 Ruth told Naomi, for whither thy goest, I will go; and where thy lodgest, I will lodge, thy people hall be my people and thy Go, my God; where thou diest will I and there will I be buried. Ru 2:11 Boaz told Ruth, It hath fully been shown me, all that thou hast done unto thy mother in law since the death of thine husband.

Ps 35:14 I bowed down heavily as one that mourneth for his mother. Prov 6:20 My son, keep thy Father's commandment and forsake not the law of thy mother. Prov 10:1 A wise son maketh a glad father but a foolish son is the heaviness of his mother. Prov 23:22 Despise not thy mother when she is old. Ezek 16:44 As is the mother, so is the daughter.

Jesus said, Matt 12:50 For whosoever shall do the will of my Father, which is in heaven, the same is my brother, my sister and mother. Matt 19:19 Honor thy father and thy mother. Mark 1:30 Simon's wife's mother lay sick of a fever, and anon they tell of her: 31 He came and took her by the hand and immediately the fever left her, and she ministered unto them.

Luke 2:48 Mary said to Jesus, why hast thou thus dealt with us? Behold thy father and I have sought thee sorrowing. Jesus said Luke 2:49 How is it that ye sought me? wist ye not that I must be about my Father's business? 50 They understood not the sayings which He spake unto them. 51 but His mother kept all thee sayings in her heart.

Jn: 19:25-27 Now there stood by the cross of Jesus His mother. When Jesus saw His mother an the disciple standing by, whom He loved, He said unto His mother, woman, behold thy son. Then said unto the disciple, behold thy mother and from that hour the disciple took her unto his own home.

Can you imagine the hurt and pain, Mary as a mother experienced when she saw her son on the cross? How would you feel if it were your son? But the love of Jesus for her, gave her another son. She continued being a mother. The disciple took her in, and I feel he loved her just as much as if she bore him. Such is love.

Should One Take Communion

Created on 2018-01-12 17:37

There is power in the blood of JESUS. Rom 3:25 say have faith in the blood of JESUS. 1 Cor 15:50-51 Flesh and blood cannot inherit the kingdom of God. Behold I show you a mystery, we shall not all sleep, but we shall all be changed. God is a SPIRIT and if His Spirit dwell within you, you are part of the church-His church which was purchased with His own blood and God says to feed the church. Acts 20:28

Eph 1:7 says we have redemption through His blood, the forgiveness, according to the riches of His grace. Are you examining yourself, prior to drinking of the cup? For 1 Cor 11:27 says wherefore whoever shall eat this bread and drink the cup of the Lord unworthily shall be guilty of the body and blood of the Lord. However JESUS said in Mark 14:24 This is my blood of the New Testament which is shed for many. 1 Cor 11:25 says this cup is the New Testament in my blood. This do ye, as oft as ye drink it, in remembrance of me. JESUS said in Mark 11:25 I say unto you I will drink no more of the fruit of the vine, until that day I drink it new in the kingdom. 1 Cor 11:26 say for as often as ye eat this bread, and drink this cup, you do show the Lord's death till He come.

My questions are as follow: Didn't He come again? Wasn't He resurrected-I believe He was-didn't He ascend to heaven and now sit on the throne to the right of the FATHER? Also isn't the bread the WORD of Jesus Christ written in the New Testament in His blood (the red ink) which we are to partake and digest to live holy and righteous and lovingly and peaceful? JESUS is the Word manifested in the flesh. Please read John 1:1-14. Why drink in remembrance of of His death when His SPIRIT is alive and dwell within us? Why when He was resurrected from the dead and have the keys of life and death in His hands and sit at the right of the Father?

I am not knocking communion-He said seek and ye shall find, knock and it will be opened and ask and it shall be given. I desire clarity and understanding of the practice as well as wisdom and knowledge. I have taken communion but sending it to me by mail for me to take is taking it a bit too far. What happen to home visits for the sick and shut ins? I am sure your response to my questions will help others with those same questions. Pray the Lord's Prayer today. Be blessed in JESUS name. AMEN.

The Spiritual Revolutionary Revival Of The Holy People Of God

Created on 2019-08-11 10:36

The Revival need to start now. Seek ye first The Kingdom Of God to enable you to receive every good thing which comes down from above from ABBA FATHER. With the United States being led by president number 45, you are experiencing all the negative features in life under his leadership. You are witnessing and experiencing Racism with a capital R, bigotry, hatred, separation, dividing and conquering, killings, financial suffering, denial of health treatments. The list goes on and on. Veteran are hungry and homeless, aid is given to the rich and the poor are being ignored, two classes of people are being set up-the have and the have not or rather the rich and the poor.

Preachers are preaching and teaching lies about him being God's anointed. You need to stop eating all the words those preachers are feeding you especially if they are not really ABBA FATHER'S disciples. Remember, satan have preachers on earth also who know the Word of God. And I am not saying he is the anti-christ, I am just saying I don't believe he is the anointed one.

It is time for the true body of Christ to pull together and have a revolutionary revival of the Holy people of God. It is time to pull together and be of service to God's people. We have to pool our resources, wisdom, knowledge money, etc. etc. and help improve the quality of living by providing homes for the homeless (especially mothers and children) providing jobs to enable one to take care of themselves and or family, provide transitional housing and help the drug addicts and alcoholics, provide screening and health care to the sick and needy, food and drink to the hungry and thirsty, financial help to the poor. Spiritual food to the hungry and thirsty, education to parents and children, general guidance and a helping hand. In other words, all of us in the body who has been given a talent or talents should use their skills and pull together to help heal our nation physically, mentally, emotionally, financially. Spiritually and in any and every way in which a healing is needed and we have skills available to do so. .

Remember, your ass gets kicked, not kissed when you do not exercise your right to vote. The wrong people end up leading you and planning and issuing the quality of life for you to live. It is now time for the Revival to start before too much more negative sugar honey ice tea happens.

Pray the Lord's Prayer today. Read the following psalms: 23rd, 125th, 100th., 91st, 119th, 139th and 37th. ABBA FATHER, in the name Of JESUS I ask that you bless and continue to bless with a hedge of protection those readers who read this from all evil, all harm, all danger, all hurt, all pain and suffering. Bless them with good health and bless them financially abundantly. Amen, Amen and Amen.

The Antichrist-The Last Days

Created on 2016-11-09 10:29

This article is not referring to anyone in general, but it has been on my mind for over a week to write it. In the last post, women I requested you to unite. How can you know when satan has entered your life through someone? How many of you know satan was a beautiful angel and a masterful musician? How many of you know he is the father of a lie? Can you recognize the characteristics of one who is doing satan's work? Are you eating fruit from the tree God told Adam and Eve not to eat from?

You know, I have a garden, a beautiful one. Several come to visit my garden. I am quite sure they noticed I keep my lawn cut short. The reason is because snakes like to lay in the grass and the grass need to be kept short so I can see them to avoid them or get rid of them. My garden is in my mind. You know, a snake appeared unto Adam and Eve telling them they may eat the fruit from the tree God told them not to eat from. That is how we can know when satan has entered our lives through someone because they will have the characteristics of a snake.

I believe we are now living in the times that were prophecised about the antichrist. 2 Tim 3:1 This know also, that in the last days perilous times shall come. Avoid godlessness, see verses 2-17. Love not the world-see 1st John 2:2-17. Verse 18: It is the last time and as ye have heard that the antichrist shall come, even now are there MANY antichrists whereby we

know it is the last time. vs 20 Ye have unction from the Holy One and ye know all things.

I have not written unto you because you know not the truth, but because ye know and no lie is in the truth. Who is a liar but he that deny that Jesus is the Christ? He is antichrist that denieth Father and Son. See vs 22-29. Set aside time, open your Spiritual mind and read the whole book of Revelation. Pray the Lord's Prayer today for it is the perfect prayer. Petition God to keep a protective hedge around us all who are His people.

note: I heard that the Artic floor has a strange sound emitting from it. google mysterious sound coming from Artic floor. I am about to do so just to see what it is about.

The Blessings For
You From Keeping
Your Appointed Time
With The Lord God

Created on 2015-09-29 23:42

Did you give your atonement offering? The day of atonement has come and gone. It was a special day for us for redemption from sin. If you obeyed in the observance of the Holy Day, God's word promised us seven blessings as well as a double portion.

If you obeyed God, you are promised a double portion from the Lord as per Joel 2:23, a double portion of every blessing of God and a second chance to succeed from what you may have failed at. Joel 2:24 a full threshing floor-be blessed financially abundantly-have an overflow. Joel 2:25 a return of what you lost given to you by angels to restore what satan has taken from you. Joel 2:26 Receive your miracles-He will deal wondrously favorably with you. Joel 2:27 we are promised Jesus divine presence in our lives. Joel 2:28 Revelation knowledge-our sons and daughters will prophesy, old men dream dreams and young men see visions. Joel 2:32 Deliverance is promised- permanent freedom. Nothing can stop or block you because God set you free.

This is also the year of the JUBILEE which happens once every fifty years. It's the year in which God declares and end to slavery and debt. Nothing can enslave you or have power over you, such as an addiction or a habit. You are also free of the spiritual debt of sin and memories of past sin.

Isaiah 55:6 Seek the Lord while He may be found, call upon Him while He is near. The feast of the tabernacles is an appointed time to be near God. You should not come empty handed. Deut 16:16. You should have an offering for strangers, orphans, the widows, those in need who are suffering and helpless. This feast will be celebrated Sunday, October 4th, 2015. Help the needy so God will release 5 supernatural blessings upon you.

OXEN-financial blessings in your livelihood, financial health and shelter.

SHEEP-day to day essentials of life- food, clothing, etc. etc.

WINE-joy- emotional and spiritual blessings.

STRONG DRINK-for healing-medical needs met.

WHATEVER YOUR SOUL DESIRES-God want to give you everything you desire and long for in your heart.

May you receive your blessings from you being obedient, not coming before God empty handed, when you kept the appointed times to be in His Presence. AMEN.

The Insurrection-What Just Happened?

Created on 2021-01-13 13:49

I believe voters thought they were choosing the lesser of two evils. However, will that lesser evil become a Spiritual Leader? Spiritual enough to lead this country into going back to being GOD'S PEOPLE? Have them turn their faces from their wicked ways, humble themselves, seek God's face and pray so God can keep His promise of healing the land and restoring prosperity?

No necessary level of force was used to stop the rioters. Looking at this race-wise, had this been a black takeover, there would have been plenty of body bags. Trump led this up-rise because he believe only white people have rights to democracy. He led the up-rising because he believe he lost because of the black vote and believed they should not have voting rights. He challenged all the areas where Biden won with the black vote. He felt if you would only count the white votes, he did win.

Now, how I feel about the white churches part in this. They believe white churches and black churches should be divided. They believed in setting up and supporting lies to erode the foundation of democracy and to overthrow the government if necessary to keep the thought of blacks as not being equal human beings alive. It is a big lie in believing the outcome of politics come down to races. Not all white churches feel this way.

The black churches are busy frowning on Moslems and Muslims who wish to call Jehovah-Allah. They believe in Jesus as their Lord and Savior. But all of their knees are not bowing. They are busy in church seeing who has on what, who is doing what, not allowing the preaching of the Holy Trinity as one or not allowing preaching of the Holy Ghost Spirit in their church.

The church on a whole is busy dividing up the body of Christ church into various denominations, such as Protestant, Evangelistic, Baptist, Roman Catholics, Jehovah Witnesses, 7 day Advent. Mormans and a host of several denominations.

Part 1 of 3 - The Word

Created on 2016-07-20 20:26

It was revealed to write on all three. Matt 4:4 Man should not live by bread alone, but by every word that proceeds out of the mouth of God. 2 Tim 3:16 All scripture is given by inspiration of God, and is profitable for doctrine, for reproof, for correction, for instruction in righteousness. There is power in the Word of God, for in the beginning was the Word, and the Word was with God, and the Word was God. The same was in the beginning with God. All things were made by Him, and without Him was not anything made that was made. John 1:1-3.

In Isa 45:5-9 God stated in His words-"I am the Lord, and there is none else, there is beside me. I girded thee though thou hast not known me; that they may know from the rising of the sun, and from the west, that there is none beside me. I make peace and create evil: I the Lord do all these things. Drop down, ye heavens, from above, and let the skies pour down Righteousness, let the earth open and let them bring forth Salvation, and let Righteousness spring together, I the Lord have created It. (Sweet Jesus). Read about the creation with His Word in Gen 1:1-31. Accept, believe and receive His Word. Here is what scripture say about His Word.

Heb 4:12 For the Word of God is quick and powerful, and sharper than any two edged sword, piercing even to the dividing asunder of soul and spirit, and of the heart, and marrow, and is a discerner of the thoughts and intents of the heart Rom 10:13 So then faith cometh by hearing, and hearing by the word of God. Acts 20:32 and now brethern, I commend you to God, and to the word of his grace, which is able to build you up, and to give you an inheritance among all them which are sanctified. 1 Thess2:13.....thank we God without ceasing, because, when ye receive the word of God.....ye received it not as the word of en, but as it is in truth, the word of God, which effectually worketh also in you that believe. 1 Pet 1:23 being born again, not of corruptible seed, but of incorruptible, by the word of God which liveth and abideth forever. 2 Tim 3:16 All scripture is given by inspiration of God, and is profitable for doctrine, for reproof, for correction, for instruction in righteousness: Jer 15:16 thy words were found and I did eat them, and thy word was unto me the joy and rejoicing of mine heart, for I am called by thy name, O Lord God of hosts. James 1:22 but be ye doers of the word, and not hearers only, deceiving your own selves. Gal 5:17 for the flesh lusteth against the Spirit and the Spirit against the flesh; and these are contrary the one to the other, so that ye cannot do the things that ye would. John 15:3 Now ye are clean through the Word which I have spoken unto you. Not only can you be cleansed by the Word but by the Blood Of Jesus in which I will submit information on in Part 2 of this post. Part 3 will be about the Spirit.

Please pray The Lord's prayer today for it is the perfect prayer giving us the words to pray coming from The Word.

Part 2 of 3 - The Blood

Created on 2016-07-25 12:50

THE BLOOD-Not only can you be cleansed by the Word but the Blood of Jesus. 1 John 1:7 But if we walk in the light, as He is in the light, we have fellowship one with another, and the blood of Jesus Christ His Son cleanseth us from ALL sin. Matt 26:28 For this is my blood of the new testament, which is shed for many for the remission of sin. Heb 9:22 and almost all things are by the law purged with blood, and without shedding of blood is no remission. Heb 9:12 Neither by the blood of goats and calves, but by his own blood He entered in once into the Holy Place, having obtained eternal redemption for us. Heb 13:20 Now the God of Peace, that brought again from the dead our Lord Jesus, that great shepherd of the sheep, through the blood of the everlasting covenant. Rev 1:5 and from Jesus Christ who is the faithful witness, and the first begotten son of he dead, and the prince of the kings of the earth. Unto Him that loved us, and washed us from our sins in His own blood.

The Blood cleansed us, redeemed us and gave us salvation. Some of us plead the blood of Jesus when we make our requests known to God. I have to be totally honest and admit I saw nowhere in the bible where we are to do such a thing when we are in a dilemma. I am not suggesting you not do it, but I am saying many of us do not know how to plead the blood. But I do know we can plead it when we are in spiritual warfare. I am currently being exposed to the knowledge, understanding and wisdom of pleading the blood.

Additional bible scriptures about The Blood are: 1 Corin11:25, Matt 26:27-28, Mark 14:23-24, Like 22:20 Heb 9:11-15 But when Christ appeared as a high priest of the good things to come. He entered through the greater and more perfect tabernacle, not made with hands, that is to say, not of this creation He entered the Holy Place for ALL. having obtained eternal redemption. For if the blood of goats and bulls and the ashes of a heifer, sprinkling the uncleaned sanctify for the purging of the flesh, how much more shall the blood of Christ, who through the eternal Spirit offered Himself without spot to God cleanse your conscience from dead works to serve the living God? and for this reason He is the Mediator of the new covenant, by means of death, for the redemption of the transgressions under the first covenant, that those who are called may receive the promise of the eternal inheritance. Acts 20:28 Be on guard for yourselves and for all the flock, among which the Holy Spirit has made you overseers, to shepherd the church of God which He purchased with His own blood.

Rev 5:9-10 and they sang a new song saying, "Worthy are you to take the book and break it seals, for You were slain, and purchased for God with Your blood from every tribe and tongue and people and nation. You have made them to be a kingdom and priests to our God; and they will reign upon the earth. Rom 5:9 Much more than having now been justified by His blood, we shall be saved from the wrath of God through Him. (see Matt 26:28 and Mark 14:24 which mentions being justified by His blood and the covenant).

Jesus overcame satan for us a;;. Rev 12:10-11 Then I heard a loud voice in heaven saying, "Now the salvation, and the power, and the kingdom of our God and the authority of His Christ have come, for the accuser of our brethern has been thrown down, he who accuses them before our God day and night." And they overcame him because of the blood of the Lamb and because of the word of their testimony, and they did not love their life even when faced with death." Rev 1:5-6 and from Jesus Christ, the faithful witness, the firstborn of the dead, and the ruler of the kings of the earth To Him who loves us and released us from our sins by His blood-and He has made us to be a kingdom, priests to His God and Father-to Him be the glory and the dominion forever and ever. Amen

Jesus willingly shed His blood for us. Afterwards, He said to us He will send us a Comforter to be with us forever. Part 3 about the Spirit will be posted 2 days from today. Please pray the Lord's Prayer today, after all it is the perfect prayer, it came from The Word - Himself. Amen.

Part 3 of 3 - The Spirit

Created on 2016-07-27 11:58

THE HOLY SPIRIT---JESUS SAID HE WOULD SEND TO US A COMFORTER TO BE WITH US FOREVER. He said the following: John 14:15-17 If you love Me you will obey what I command. And I will ask the Father and He will give you another Comforter to be with you forever-The Spirit of Truth. The world cannot accept him because it neither sees him nor knows him. But you know him for he lives with you and will be in you. John 14:25-26 All this I have spoken while still with you, but the Comforter, the Holy Spirit whom the father will send in my name, will teach you all things and will remind you of everything I have said to you. When the Comforter comes, whom I will send to you from the Father, He will testify about Me. John 16:7-8 But I will tell you the truth: it is for your good that I am going away. Unless I go away, the Comforter will not come to you, but if I go I will send him unto you. When he comes he will convict the world of guilt in regards to sin and righteousness and judgement.......John 16:13-15 But when he, the Spirit of Truth comes, he will guide you into all truth. He will not speak on his own, he will speak only what he hears, and he will tell you what is yet to come. He will bring glory to me by taking from what is Mine and making it known to you. All that belongs to the Father is mine. That is why I said the Spirit will take from what is Mine and make it known to you.

John 7:38-39 He who believes in Me, as the scripture said, 'From his innermost being will flow rivers of living water.' But this He spoke of the Spirit, whom those who believed in Him were to receive, for the Spirit was not yet given, because Jesus was not yet glorified. Acts 2:33 Therefore having been exalted to the right hand of God, and having received from the Father the promise of the Holy Spirit, He has poured forth this which you both see and hear. John 14:16-18 I will ask the Father and He will give to you another Helper, that He may be with you forever, that is the Spirit of Truth, whom the world cannot receive, because it does not see Him or know Him, but you know because He abides with you and will be in you. "I will not leave you as orphans, I will come to you." Romans 8:16 The Spirit Himself testifies with our spirit that we are children of God, Ephesians 3:16 that He would grant you, according to the riches of His Glory, to be strengthened with power through His Spirit in the inner man..

Seek, knock, ask, you will be answered. I also believe it is not necessary to repeat a prayer request to the Father over and over. He heard your request the first time so only ask Him one time. He also said you have not because you ask not but He knows before you ask because He knows the spirit of your heart. Also stop living carnally. Be your higher self and live spiritually. Galatians 5:17 says for the flesh lust against the Spirit and the Spirit against the flesh; and these are contrary, the one to the other so that ye cannot do the things that ye would. When the will of God and the will of man are one, then the world will accept the fact that the resurrection of Jesus Christ happened: we were ALL washed clean, redeemed and have salvation, and the glory of God will be something to behold.

Know also The Comforter is The Spirit of Truth, our Counselor, our Advocate...........Does the Spirit of Truth dwell within you? Examine yourself, are you still telling little lies to spare someone the truth about a situation or spare their feelings? The Comforter is The Holy Spirit. He IS NOT a man as some of us are being told. Re-read your scripture about the Holy Spirit. When the Comforter dwell within you, you will get a taste of the salvation and glory The Father has for those who love Him and dwell in Jesus. The Holy Spirit is the Spirit of God which He gives to true believers. I am going to end now asking you to PRAY the Lord's Prayer. TO GOD BE THE GLORY. HALLELUJAH. AMEN, AMEN AND THANK GOD, IN THE NAME OF JESUS.

Today, Help Me Magnify His Name

Created on 2017-07-18 12:28

Let us praise God. Please help me magnify His name today. Let us exalt His name. Let us sing praises to Him today and everyday. Glory, glory, glory to God Our Father, our Lord, our Savior, our Friend. Rev 4:11 Thou art worthy O Lord to receive glory and honor and power: for thou has created all things, and for thy pleasure they are and were created. Rev 5:12 Worthy is the Lamb that was slain to receive power and riches and wisdom and strength and honor and glory and blessing. Rev 4:8 Holy, Holy, HolyLord God Almighty, which was and is and is to come.

Let us glorify Him now, today, tonight tomorrow, always. He means so much to us. There are countless ways in which we can have intimacy with Him. We awaken this morning with His Holy Breath going through our bodies. It is a good thing to give thanks unto the Lord and to sing praises unto the name of The Most High.

Thou, Lord, has made me glad through thy work: I will triumph in the works of thy hands. O Lord, how great are thy works AND thy thoughts are very deep. Those that be planted in your house shall flourish in your courts. They shall bring forth fruit in old age. Lord you are upright, you are my rock and there is no unrighteousness in you. Lord, you reign. You are clothe with majesty and with strength. Your throne is established of old. You are from everlasting. Lord God, you are mightier than all which can or cannot be imagined. Holiness become thine house, O Lord; and I shall dwell in your house singing praises to you forever. Lord Jesus I thank you. Amen and Amen.

Jesus is saying in Rev 3:20-21 Behold, I stand at the door and knock. If any man hear my voice and open the door, I will come in and sup with him and he with me. To him that overcome will I grant to sit with me in my throne even as I also overcame and am set down with my Father in His throne. He that have an ear, let him hear what the Spirit is saying. Pray the Lord's Prayer today and everyday. It is the perfect prayer. It is the prayer Jesus taught us to pray in Matthew 6:9-13. May every reader receive blessings today.

Walk In The Light
Instead Of Darkness

Created on 2016-05-16 04:11

Isa 43:21 This people have I formed for myself: they shall show forth my praise. Jam 2:26 for as the body without the spirit is dead, so faith without works is dead. Rev 14:9-10 If any man worship the beast and his image, and receive his mark in his forehead or in his hand, they shall drink of the wine of the wrath of God. Rev 21:5 Behold I make all things new.

Gen 1:1 For in the beginning God created the heaven and the earth. And man sinned so greatly, God destroyed all but 8 people. He made all things new. Gen 1:9 God said let the waters gather together unto one place, and let the dry land appear. God said Gen 9:13 I do set my bow in the cloud and it shall be a token of a covenant between me an the earth. Gen 9:15 I will remember my covenant and the waters shall no more become a flood to destroy all flesh.

In the beginning Gen 1:16 God made two great lights, the greater light to rule the day and the lesser light to rule the night; he made the stars also. Col 1:16 For by Him were all things created, that are in heaven and that are in earth, visible and invisible, all things were created by Him and for HIM. Gen 1:3 and God said let there be light, and there was light.

Luke 11:35 Take heed therefore that the light which is in thee be not darkness. Eph 5:8 for ye were sometimes darkness, but now are ye light in the LORD, walk as children of light. Rom 13:12 Let us therefore cast off the work of darkness and let us put on the armour of light. John 3:36 He that believeth in the Son hath everlasting life, and he that believeth not the Son, shall not see life, but the wrath of God abide on him. John 1:4-5 In Him was life and the life was the light of men and the Light shineth in darkness, and darkness comprehended it not.

Rev 21:6 I am ALPHA and OMEGA, the beginning and the end. I will give unto him that is athirst of the fountain of the water of life freely. PS 12:16 The Words of the LORD are pure WORDS; as silver tried in the furnace of the earth, purified seven times. AMEN.

We Can Have What We Say

Created on 2017-10-22 14:56

Readers, remember, WE ARE THE CHURCH. Today I want to do something different. As per Mark 11:22-23 I want to pray for health, healing, strength, prosperity and long life for us until we go to the grave. As per Romans 4:17 I want to call those things which do not exist as though they did. You must believe those things which are said will come to pass and have no doubt for you shall have whatsoever was said. Jesus said "Therefore, I say unto you whatsoever ye desire, when ye pray, believe that ye receive them and ye shall have them." v 24. Proverbs 18:21 says death and life are in the power of the tongue so I speak long life unto us. We shall have a long life with good health, healing, strength, prosperity and hope. Matthew 21:22 whatsoever ye ask in prayer, believe ye shall receive it, so I am asking and believing we all shall have very good health. I am believing we all shall be healed in every way we need to be healed. I am believing it shall be done. Also if two or more of us touch and agree when we ask, and we ask in the name of JESUS, JESUS said it shall be done by His Father which is in heaven.

Isaiah 55:11 So shall my word be that goeth forth out of my mouth: it shall not return unto me void; but it shall accomplish that which I please and it shall prosper in the thing whereto I sent it. Believe it. In preaching the light of God II Corinthians 4:3-4 if our gospel be hid, it is hid to them that are lost.....in whom the god of this world hath blinded the minds of them which believe not. vs 6 God who commanded the light to shine out of darkness, hath shined in our hearts, to give the light of the knowledge of the glory of God in the face of Jesus Christ. 13 We having the same spirit of faith, according as it is written I believe, therefore I have spoken, we also believe and therefore speak. vs 18 while we look not at things which are seen but at the things which are not seen; for the things which are seen are temporal but the things which are not seen are eternal.

Matt 12:34-37.......out of the abundance of the heart the mouth speaks. A good man out of the good treasure of the heart bring forth good things and an evil man of evil treasure bring forth evil things; however every idle word that man shall speak they shall give account for; for by thy words they shall be justified and by thy words they shall be condemned. Rom 10:17 faith cometh by hearing and hearing the word of God. Ez 12:25, 28 In these verses He states for I AM the LORD. I will speak and the word I shall speak shall come to pass; it shall be no more prolonged, for in your days........will I say the word and will perform it saith the Lord. Gen 1:1-31 and God said Let there be......see Ez 37:1-10. God hath chosen the foolish things of the world to confound the wise and God hath chosen the weak things of the world to confound the things which are mighty.........God hath chosen the things which are not to bring to nought things that are...........

Before I close I want to remind you of James 5:13-16, if you are afflicted-pray. If you are sick- call for the elders of the church (remember we are the church). We should pray over the sick and anoint them with oil in the name of the Lord. The prayers of faith shall save the sick, and the Lord shall raise him up and if he has committed sins, they shall be forgiven.......... The effective fervent prayer of a righteous man availeth much. 3 John 2-4 Beloved, I wish above all things that thou mayest prosper and be in health even as thy soul prosper. Jer17:7 Blessed is the man that trust in the Lord, and whose hope the Lord is. Heb 11:1, 3 Faith is the substance of things hoped for, the evidence of things not seen. Through faith we understand the worlds were formed by the word of God, so that things which are seen were not made of things which do appear. Isaiah 44:6 thus said the Lord........I am the first and I am the last; and beside me there is no god. 8.......yea, there is no god; I know not any. Isaiah 41:10 Fear thou not; for I am with thee; be not dismayed; for I am thy God; I will strengthen thee; yea I will help thee; yea I will uphold thee with the right hand of my righteousness. see 41:11-13.

Speak good words over and into you life and the lives of loved ones today. Speak positive words and words of love and truth. For there is rejoicing when you walk in truth. There is no greater joy then to hear that God's children walk in truth. Pray the Lord's Prayer today and everyday. God bless you.

What Gift Did
You Receive

Created on 2017-02-08 11:38

Do you know what your gift is as a member in the body of Christ? In this post I have tried to point out the gifts we receive from God, Jesus and the Holy Spirit. Remember, God gave us the gift of life and what we do with it is our gift to Him. Jesus gave us the gift of the Comforter-the Holy Spirit.

These are some of the gifts of God: Ecc 3:13 every man should eat and drink and enjoy the good of all his labour, it is the gift of God. Rom 6:23 the gift of God is eternal life through Jesus Christ our Lord. Eph 2:8 For by grace ye are saved through faith, another gift of God. James 1:17 Every good gift and every perfect gift is from above, and cometh down from the Father.........

1 Cor 12:1-14 There are diversities of gifts by the same Spirit and there are differences of administration but the same God and there are diversities of operations but it is the same God which worked all in all. But the manifestation of the Spirit is given to every man to profit withal. For to one is given by the Spirit the word of wisdom, to another the word of knowledge by the same Spirit, to another - faith by the same Spirit, to another the gifts of healing by the same Spirit, to another the working of miracles, to another prophecy, to another discerning of Spirits, to another divers kinds of tongues, to another the interpretation of tongues but all these worketh that one and the selfsame Spirit, dividing to every man severally as He will.

The body is not one member but many but the body is one and hath many members, and all the members of that body being many are one body for by one Spirit we are all baptized into one body whether he be Jews or Gentiles, bond or free, we have been all made to drink into one Spirit.

The perfect gift-1 Corin14:1 Follow after charity and desire Spiritual gifts that ye may prophesy for he that speaketh in an unknown tongue speaketh NOT unto men but unto GOD, for no man understandeth him. In the Spirit he speak mysteries.

Eph 4:4-8, read 11-14 There is one body and one spirit even as ye are called in one hope of your calling; one Lord, one faith, one baptism. One God and Father of all, who is above all, through all and in you ALL. But unto everyone of us is given grace according to the measure of the gift of Christ. When He ascended up on high. He gave gifts to men. He gave some apostles, and some prophets and some evangelists and some pastors and teachers for the perfecting of the saints, for the work of the ministry for the edifying of the body of Christ. Take a moment to pray The Lord's Prayer when you finish reading this post. God bless each and every one of you.

Witchcraft-The
Problem In My Life

Created on 2017-06-20 11:34

Prayer works. All power, all power belong to God, ABBA FATHER. By us being on one accord, touching and agreeing, those of you whom I asked to pray and ask God to handle problems, I found we received favorable results.

In Micah 2:1 it is written, woe to them that devise iniquity, and work evil upon their beds; when the morning is light, they practice it, because it is in the power of their hand.

There was a woman in my life who used to live in my home, who used my computer to call on the power of darkness. When I tried to use my computer, the cursor traveled all over the page. I had to buy a new computer. She visited my home, after she moved continuously, sometimes spending the night, eating food I prepared, making me feel as though she was attempting to take over my home. She and her mate even used my address as their address to receive mail such as letters and packages regularly.

On one of her visits when I was asleep, she dressed my front door steps. My next door neighbor removed the dressing by washing my steps down continuously. She dressed the doors on the first level of my home and also those in the basement. I removed every thing with holy oil. Because I am a firm believer in our Lord and Savior Jesus Christ, Jehovah and the Holy Ghost Spirit, whatever craft she tried to do against me did not work. ABBA FATHER has a hedge of protection around me, my family and loved ones and all that I own.

I know the craft exist. People are free to practice whatever they choose to believe in or even feel free not to believe in anyone but themselves. That is a personal choice, but don't try to force your belief on me or subject me to have to accept you and your practices...I am not a religious person. I am a Spiritual person having the Spirit of Jesus Christ dwell within me so I prayed and believed in the power of praying Psalms 91 and 23.

Wholeness reigns with me now-not brokenness. The Lord God I serve, ABBA FATHER, does not let death and darkness rule in my life. I place my trust in Jesus, in doing so I now have love, peace and beauty in my life. She no longer have access to my home and I no longer have to listen to her blaspheming the Holy Ghost Spirit, Jesus, Jehovah, Allah, Buddha or any other deity other people chose to pray to.

My home now has been restored to its former beauty. It is filled with peace, love, laughter and good feelings and prayer. I thank Jesus. Pray the Lord's prayer today and be blessed.

Women For Equality

Created on 2015-09-14 11:52

I don't know what is going on, but I feel JEHOVAH is using what little skills I have to speak out against all ills and injustice occurring. To all women for equality, men who support us and young adults, let's get together, start using your voting power, economic power and try to correct the ills and injustices occurring.

Mark 9:23 states if thou canst believe, all things are possible to him that believeth. Mark 11:24 states therefore I say unto you, whatsoever ye desire, when ye pray, believe that ye receive them, and ye shall have them. Matt 18:18 states whatsoever ye bind on earth shall be bound in heaven, and whatsoever ye loose on earth shall be loosed in heaven. Let us bind up all the ills, injustice and wars. Let us loose help, love, wisdom, understanding and life with good quality. Matt 18:19 states if two of you shall agree on earth as touching anything that they shall ask, it shall be done for them of my Father which is in heaven.

We need to work when we use our faith. We must get together and pull together to correct the problems of the elderly, disabled, children and babies, sick and shut in, homelessness, abused, suicidal, hungry & poverty, innocent people behind bars. Let's correct the social problems, the economic problems, religious problems, health problems, political problems, etc. etc.

It starts by us voting into office those people with skills, wisdom, understanding and compassion to correct the problems. Also encourage the young adults to exercise their voting right power. It starts by us controlling what is being done with our money (even if it means starting our own financial institution). We need to manage how we spend our money better. Is a bottle of alcohol or drugs more important than a loaf of bread, bottle of milk or can of beans to feed hungry children? Come on now, let's get out priorities right!!!!!!!

We put our money into institutions who refuse to lend to us when we get in a crunch. We are working for pay which is below a minimum wage which is too low for a family of one to exist, not just one of 3-4 people. Women have equal knowledge and skills as their men counterparts and a e still settling for less wages just to say they have a job. Don't settle. Start your own business in the same field you have expertise in. We have global warming starting to destroy the world, fires in California and floods in other states. Hurricanes and Tornadoes, shortage of crops for food, etc. etc.

Let us pull together and work together to solve some of these problems. I mentioned two of several ways it can be done; by voting and economically. Would you like to see or settle for financial institutions or two or three super rich families ruling the world and controlling everything? Come on people-wake up- take control of destiny. Get on the straight and narrow path. Stop branching off in all directions.

Be obedient, keep the statutes and commandments of God. Deut 4:6-7 keep therefore and do them for this is your wisdom and understanding in the sight of nations, which shall hear all these statutes and say, surely this great nation is a wise and understanding people. For what nation is there so great, who hath God so nigh unto thee, as the LORD our God is in all things that we call upon him for?

Come on All women for equality, men who support them, young adults and people in general regardless of political affiliation, religious affiliation, social standings, race, creed, nationality: let's come together and work on a change for the better, for the world and the people in it.

I will close now by enclosing my latest poem:

Wisdom and understanding goes hand in hand, on a man's search for knowledge in this land, Knowledge will welcome you into her embrace, but wisdom and understanding should be your chase. With the two of them, you can go far. Lift both hands up, just reach for that star. Be happy, for with that star comes love, and you'll find it's blessed by God above.

Women Unite-Let's Assert Ourselves

Created on 2016-10-23 20:29

Because Society has been controlled by a patriarch ruler-ship, some men deem it okay to be disrespectful to women. I'm sure I am going to piss a few people off, however, a religious mindset that is nothing more than a patriarch light-code have for some reason taken women out of the equation of and with creation.

Women appear to be under attack all over the world now. Enough is enough. Let's stop accepting and allowing bullshit. Yep, I said it. It's time to remove the veil from your eyes and see what is happening and know what type of behavior and conversation you will no longer accept because you don't have to.

Women are the backbone of this world, yet they are being treated as though they are low-class people. You must remember most women are creators, especially since they give birth to men; some are the very ones who end up disrespecting and abusing women. We are the first god your face see when you are born. After all God is in us and we are in HIM.

Where did you learn to disrespect woman? Was it in your home, your school, your place of worship, your community, your job, your business your government, just where? Why do you as men allow your mother, grandmother, sister, aunt, niece or other female relative be disrespected, abused, attacked verbally and physically and emotionally and mentally? Why do you accept it? What do you do about it? Why are children and young adults now allowed to do the same and cause grownups to fear them?

Women, become educated to have a quality life. Be your higher self. Live with love, truth, peace, freedom and justice. Our rights are daily being taken away. We can't even spank our children anymore without the threat of child abuse being held over our heads.. What does the bible say about sparing the rod?

Mothers unite. You are the creator. That man child came down from between your legs. You manifested that life being seem in this world. You have a number one position in his life. It's a lie when they say a woman can't raise a man to be a man. She can instill values in him to treat a woman as a mother, lady and or queen. Someone to be loved and cared for, with dignity and respect. If that woman does not know how to be a woman herself, it is not your place to teach her how. Let her turn to a woman of wisdom, knowledge and understanding to teach her how. Do your part spiritually, emotionally, mentally, physically, financially, sexually and any other positive "lly". Do not be negative. Do not be abusive verbally, physically or mentally.

Wife in being a submissive person, God-in-you know you don't have to be stupid about it. God did not put you under man's feet. He put satan there. God put you beside your man to walk and live accordingly. Sister be an assertive sibling. Have your brother and the men in your life treat you with the respect you deserve. Carry yourself as a lady and or a queen.

While we are the subject of disrespect, women you need to stop disrespecting women also, especially if you intend to be a potential daughter-in-law. Young woman, it is not your place to compete for the love of a man against his mother. It is also not your place to try and be his mother or to try and take her place as the woman in his life. Respect the fact that she gave birth to him. He is a fruit from her tree, an extension of her. She want him to find a mate, be fruitful and multiply like it is written. It is not your place to try and raise him or to teach him to be a man. If you can not be a friend first and love, trust and respect him as the man he is, be grown enough to leave him alone. He deserve a woman who knows how to carry herself as a woman, friend, lady, queen and mate.

WOMEN UNITE. Unite in a positive manner and as a positive force to live and deal with.